IN 1345 the bubonic plague of Asia broke out in Europe. During the next three years it swept across the Continent, reaching England in 1348. At least a third of the people alive at the time died amid fearful suffering and distress. It was a human disaster on a scale never known before in history.

The consequences of the plague were important and far-reaching. Labour became scarce, land was plentiful, prices rose; the old manorial system went into rapid decline. Among rural people, who formed most of the population, there were implanted bitter discontents. These found expression in the Peasants' Revolt of 1381, when London lay at the mercy of the mob, and the whole of medieval society seemed in danger of collapse.

This book reconstructs these two great events in English history by means of extracts from chronicles, sermons, court records, pamphlets, poems and other writings by men who lived at this time, some of whom died as the result of plague or violence. Illustrated throughout with contemporary pictures, this new DOCUMENTARY HISTORY title provides a unique and authentic study of this shattering period of medieval life.

DR. LEONARD W. COWIE is Senior Lecturer in History at Whitelands College, Putney, and a Fellow of the Royal Historical Society. One of his main interests is the impact of religion in history. His books include *About the Bible, Seventeenth-Century Europe, Eighteenth-Century Europe, Hanoverian England, The March of the Cross, The Reformation, Luther, Plague and Fire,* and *The Pilgrim Fathers.*

*Frontispiece* The Army of the dead. Victims of the
Black Death attacking a living town.

# The Black Death and Peasants' Revolt

Leonard W. Cowie

*"When Adam delved, and Eve span,
Who was then the gentleman?"*
*Text of John Ball's revolutionary
sermon at Blackheath during the
Peasants' Revolt, 1381.*

*In this series*

ISBN 0 85340 167 5
Copyright © 1972 by Wayland (Publishers) Ltd
49 Lansdowne Place, Hove, East Sussex BN3 1HF
2nd impression 1981
Printed by The Garden City Press Limited
Letchworth, Hertfordshire SG6 1JS

# Contents

# The Illustrations

# 1, A Troubled England

TOGETHER WITH the rest of Europe, England suffered during the fourteenth century a terrible outbreak of plague (commonly known as the Black Death), which was followed by a wave of peasant unrest. These events produced important social changes. English society then was based upon the principle that there were three main classes of people, each with its own purpose to fulfil. These were the clergy, the nobility, and the peasants—in other words those who prayed, fought, and worked.

*Praying, fighting and working*

The peasants were by far the largest group; it was accepted that they supported the other two classes by their labours. Even the saintly Raymon Lull could write: "It is seemly that men should plow and dig and work hard that the earth may yield the fruits from which the knight and his horse will live; and that the knight who rides and does a lord's work should get his wealth from the things on which his men are to spend much toil and fatigue (1)."

The Church and the nobility owned great estates, to which the peasants were bound as serfs. In return for their own small plots of land, these serfs had to do work on their lord's land. The French chronicler Jean Froissart explained: "It is the custom in England, as in other countries, for the nobility to have great power over the common people, who are their serfs. This means that they are bound by law and custom to plough the fields of their masters, harvest the corn, gather it into barns, and thresh and winnow the grain. They must also mow and carry home the hay, cut and collect wood, and perform all manner of tasks of this kind. The peasants have to perform these duties by law, and they are more numerous in England than anywhere else. Thus the nobility and clergy are

*Lords and serfs*

11

*Opposite* The peaceful medieval countryside before the arrival of the Black Death

Peasants haymaking in the fields

served by right (2)."

*Serfdom upheld*  So far was serfdom accepted, that it was upheld not just on practical grounds but also for moral and religious reasons. An early twelfth-century French writer said: "Servitude is ordained by God, either because of the sins of those who become serfs, or as a trial, in order that those who are thus humbled may be made better. For servitude is of great help to religion in protecting humility, the guardian of all virtues . . . It would seem to be pride for anyone to wish to change that condition which has been given him for good reason by the divine ordinance (3)."

*God's calling*  The medieval Church told the serfs to look on their life as a calling from God. They must accept it as willingly as any other men in different positions in the world. One day, a certain monk decided to rescue his sister from being a serf. St. Anselm of Laon told him not to: "What concern is it of monks—men who have resolved to flee the world—what does it matter to them, who serves whom in the world, or under what name? Is not ever man born to labour as a bird to flight? Does not almost every man serve either under the name of lord or serf? And is not he who is called a serf in the Lord, the Lord's freeman; and he who is called free, is he not Christ's serf? So if all men labour and serve, and the serf is a freeman of the Lord, and the freeman is a serf of Christ, what does it matter apart from

12

Land workers were in short supply once the plague reached Europe

pride—either to the world or to God—who is called a serf and who is called free? (4)"

Landlords were supposed to treat their serfs fairly and protect them from injustice; but many did not. Cardinal Jacques de Vitry wrote: "Many say nowadays, when they are rebuked for having taken a cow from a poor peasant: 'Let it suffice the boor that I have left him the calf and his own life. I might do him far more harm if I would; I have taken his goose, but left him the feathers' (5)." *Harsh landlords*

Despite its high ideals, medieval society was marred by a streak of cruelty and callousness. This was displayed even by those who should have upheld those ideals. Froissart told how Edward, the Black Prince—believed to be a model of chivalry in warfare—mercilessly sacked the French city of Limoges in 1370, furious that the city had been betrayed to the French: "It was great pity to see the men, women and children that kneeled down on their knees before the Prince for mercy. But he was so inflamed with ire that he took no heed to them, so that none was heard, but all put to death, as they were met withal, and such as were nothing culpable. There was no pity taken of the poor people, who wrought never no manner of treason, yet they bought it dearer than the great personages, such as had done the evil and trespass. *Slaughter of innocents*

"There was not so hard a heart within the city of Limoges, an if

13

A conquering army sacks a medieval town. The inhabitants could expect
little mercy from the soldiers as they killed and looted

he had any remembrance of God, but that wept piteously for the
great mischief that they saw before their eyen: for more than three
thousand men, women and children were slain and beheaded that
day. God have mercy on their souls, for I trow they were
martyrs . . . (6)"

*Violent age*    This was an extreme case of brutality; but life as a whole was not
peaceful. Death and suffering were frequent in everyday life. The
common people felt a contempt for the law, and would often resort

14

Men like these alchemists tried many elaborate ways of turning metal into gold

to violence. On the death of the great-uncle of Geoffrey Chaucer in November, 1336, a London coroner remarked: "The jurors say that Simon Chaucer and one Robert de Upton, skinner . . . after dinner, quarrelled with one another in the high street opposite to the shop of the said Robert, in the said parish, by reason of rancour previously had between them, whereupon Simon wounded Robert on the upper lip; which John de Upton, son of Robert, perceiving, he took up a 'dorbarre', without the consent of his father, and

A doctor feels the pulse of a plague victim. Notice the sweet-smelling
pomander held to the doctor's nose to avoid infection

struck Simon on the left hand and side, and on the head, and then
fled into the church of St. Mary of Aldermarichirche; and in the
night following he secretly escaped from the same. He had no
chattels. Simon lived, languishing, till the said Tuesday, when he
died of the blows, early in the morning . . . The Sheriffs are ordered
to attach [arrest] the said John when he can be found in their
bailiwick . . . (7)"

Medieval writers often said that Englishmen were exceptionally violent. John Trevisa held that their aggressiveness won them victory in overseas wars at the cost of unrest and disorder at home: "English men may not be overcome in strange lands, but in their own country they be *lightliche* overcome. These men despise their own, and praise other men's, and never be content with their own estate. What befalls and belongs to other men, they will gladly take to themselves. That is why a yeoman dresses himself as a squire, a squire as a knight, a knight as a duke, and a duke as a king (8)." *Aggressive English*

Not only was death everywhere common, but the chances of saving life were generally slender. Medical science did not flourish in the Middle Ages. The efforts of most doctors were usually ill-informed and futile. This was the stock-in-trade of the alchemist in Chaucer's *Canterbury Tales* (9): *The alchemist*

> *Water in rubefaction; bullock's gall,*
> *Arsenic, brimstone, sal ammoniac,*
> *And herbs that I could mention by the sack,*
> *Moonwort, valerian, agrimony and such.*

Nor were qualified doctors any better. This is one of their remedies for a wound: "Take 4 lb. of virgin wax and resolve it in a woman's milk that beareth a knave child and do thereto afterward an ounce of mastic and an ounce of frankincense, and let them boil well together till it be well y-mellyd [mixed], and then do it off the fire and in the doing a down look thou have y-broke half a pound of tormentille well y-powdered all ready, and cast therein, and stir all-a-way without boiling till it be cold, and then take up that floateth above and smear thine hand with oil or with fresh butter and bear it again to the fire as thou wilt bear wax, till it be well y-mellid, and do therewith as thou wilt (10)." *A doctor's remedy*

Medicine was hopelessly mixed up with magic. Ritual was common, much of it surviving from ancient pagan leechcrafts. The Church condemned all who observed certain rites, or made incantations "in the gathering of medicinal herbs; save only with the Creed and the Paternoster in honour of God and our Lord". But this is an example, taken from an old medical treatise in the British Museum, of the sort of incantation that doctors used: "Mighty art thou, Queen of the Gods! thee, O Goddess, I adore in thy godhead, and on thy name do I call; vouchsafe now to fulfil *Medicine and magic*

17

my prayer, and I will give thee thanks, O Goddess, with the faith that thou hast deserved. Hear, I beseech thee, and favour my prayers; vouchsafe to me, O Goddess, that for which I now pray to thee; grant freely to all nations upon earth all herbs that thy majesty bringeth to life, and suffer me thus to gather this thy medicine. Come to me with thy healing powers (11)."

*God's punishment*     Medieval medicine little understood the causes of disease or its cure. Disease was often seen as God's punishment for sin. When an individual fell ill, he was thought to have deserved it because of his past misdeeds; if plague killed thousands of people, it must surely be due to the special wickedness of the age.

Henry of Knighton, a canon of Leicester, wrote of the days before the coming of the Black Death: "In those days [1348] there arose a huge rumour and outcry among the people, because when tournaments were held, almost in every place, a band of women would come as if to share the sport, dressed in divers and marvellous dresses of men—sometimes to the number of forty or sixty ladies, of the fairest and comeliest (though I say not of the best) among the whole kingdom. Thither they came in party-coloured tunics, one colour or pattern on the right side and another on the left, with short hoods that had pendants like ropes wound round their necks, and belts thickly studded with gold or silver—nay, they even wore, in pouches slung across their bodies, those knives which are called *daggers* in the vulgar tongue; and thus they rode on choice war horses or other splendid steeds to the place of tournament. There and thus they spent and lavished their possessions, and wearied their bodies with fooleries and wanton buffoonery, if popular report lie not . . .

"But God in this matter, as in all others, brought marvellous remedy; for He harassed the places and times appointed for such vanities by opening the floodgates of heaven with rain and thunder and lurid lightning, and by unwonted blasts of tempestuous winds... That same year and the next came the general mortality throughout the world (12)."

How terrible this mortality would be, few people can have guessed.

# 2 The Plague from the East

THE BLACK DEATH originated in the East. During 1346 rumours reached Europe of strange and terrible happenings in the East. Since few travellers went there, eyewitness accounts have not survived. But other writings are not lacking in imagination or vividness. For example, a Flemish priest, basing his remarks on a letter from a friend at the papal court, declared: "In the East, hard by Greater India, in a certain province, horrors and unheard of tempests overwhelmed the whole province for the space of three days. On the first day there was a rain of frogs, serpents, lizards, scorpions, and many venomous beasts of that sort. On the second, thunder was heard, and lightning and sheets of fire fell upon the earth, mingled with hail stones of marvellous size; which slew almost all, from the greatest even to the least. On the third day there fell fire from heaven and stinking smoke, which slew all that were left of men and beasts, and burned up all the cities and towns in those parts.

*Calamities in the East*

"By these tempests the whole province was infected; and it is conjectured that, through the foul blast of wind that came from the South, the whole seashore and surrounding lands were infected, and are waxing more and more poisonous from day to day ... (13)"

*A fatal cloud*

This idea that the plague was caused by a corrupted cloud of mist or smoke, which destroyed the land it passed over, became widely accepted. It was to influence the attempts of physicians to deal with it. Some writers thought that this cloud had been drawn up by the sun from the stagnant depths of the sea. But a chronicler from Este in Italy thought otherwise: "Between Cathay and Persia there rained a vast rain of fire, falling in flakes like snow and burning

19

*Overleaf* The triumph of death

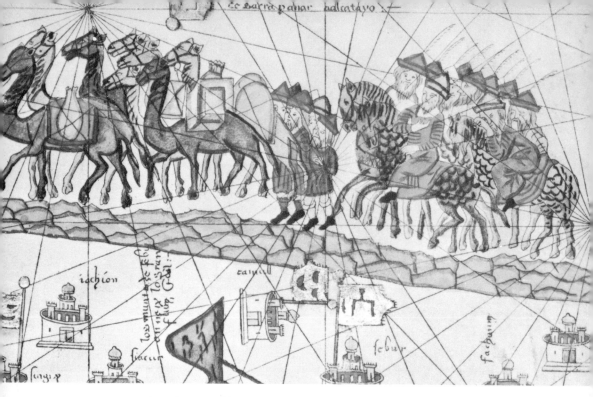

Merchants trading with the East brought the plague with them to Europe

up mountains and plains and other lands, with men and women. And then arose vast masses of smoke, and whosoever beheld this died within the space of half a day, and likewise any man or woman who looked upon those who had seen this . . . (14)"

*Rumours of death*

The origin of the plague remained a mystery; but people soon realized that a plague of unexampled fury had struck the East. Tales began to circulate, beginning in the leading European sea-ports, of the terrible numbers who were dying of it: "India was depopulated, Tartary, Mesopotamia, Syria, Armenia were covered with dead bodies; the Kurds fled in vain to the mountains. In Caramania and Caesarea none were left alive . . . (15)"

At first the news caused little concern in Europe. Stories of natural disasters from the East were common enough. But before the end of 1346 it was said that the plague was rapidly spreading westward, taking a huge toll of life as it went. Knighton recalled the fears of those days: "In this year there was a general mortality among men throughout the whole world. It broke out first in India, and spread thence in Tharsis, thence to the Saracens, and at last to the Christians and Jews; so that in the space of a single year, namely, from Easter to Easter, as it was rumoured at the court of Rome, 8,000 legions of men perished in those distant regions, besides Christians ... (16)"

We do not know how, and when, the plague first reached Europe. *Europe* The infection was probably carried along the trade routes, parti- *infected* cularly those by which Eastern spices and silks were taken to European traders. Much of this trade was carried in galleys from collecting places in the Crimea to Genoa, Venice, Messina and other Italian ports.

At any rate, by the spring of 1348 the Black Death was well established in Sicily and on the Italian mainland. Here is an account of its arrival in one of these ports by a Flemish chronicler: "In January of the year 1348, three galleys put in at Genoa, driven by a fierce wind from the East, horribly infected and laden with a variety of spices and other valuable goods. When the inhabitants of Genoa learned this, and saw how suddenly and irremediably they infected other people, they were driven forth from that port by burning arrows and divers engines of war; for no man dared touch them; nor was any man able to trade with them, for if he did he would be sure to die forthwith. Thus, they were scattered from port to port . . . (17)"

The Black Death—like the Great Plague which ravaged London *Fearful* in 1666—was bubonic plague. The germs were spread by rat fleas— *symptoms* rats were common aboard trading ships. Though no one understood this at the time, their accounts of the physical symptoms of the disease leave no doubt as to the nature of the plague. There was the tell-tale sign known as the bubo—the inflamed swelling of lymphatic glands, especially in the victim's groin or armpit.

This is how Boccaccio described them in the *Decameron*, a book of stories said to have been told by seven Florentine ladies and gentlemen, while taking refuge in a country villa to escape the plague in the city: "In men and women alike it first betrayed itself by the emergence of certain tumours in the groin or the armpits, some of which grew as large as a common apple, others as an egg, some more, some less, which the common folk called *gavocciolo*. From the two said parts of the body this deadly *gavocciolo* soon began to propagate and spread itself in all directions indifferently;

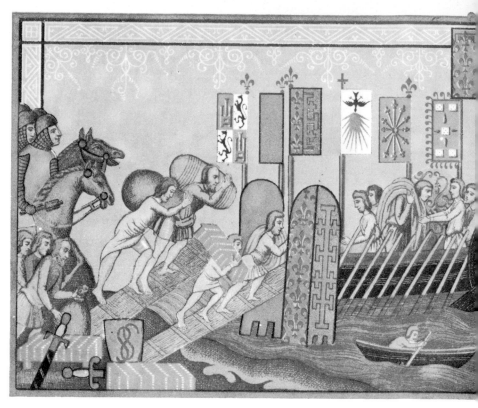

Medieval people thought that the Black Death was caused by bad air;

after which the form of the malady began to change, black spots or livid making their appearance in many cases on the arm or the thigh or elsewhere, now few and large, now minute and numerous. And as the *gavocciolo* had been and still was an infallible token of approaching death, such also were these spots on whomsoever they shewed themselves . . . (18)"

*Bubonic and pneumonic plague*

Some writers noted a variant of the plague. This was pneumonic plague, an attack of bubonic plague in which the sufferer developed pneumonia. This was a much more violent and deadly form of the disease. It seems to have come with the winter months and died out again in the spring. Gui de Chauliac, physician to the papal court at Avignon, noted these two forms of the plague: "The mortality . . . lasted seven months. It was of two types. The first lasted two months, with continuous fever and spitting of blood, and from

reality trading ships and galleys often carried rats whose fleas caused the disease

this one died in three days. The second lasted for the rest of the period, also with continuous fever but with apostumes and carbuncles on the external parts, principally on the armpits and groin. From this one died in five days . . . Men suffer in their lungs and breathing and whoever have these corrupted, or even slightly attacked, cannot by any means escape nor live beyond two days (19)."

Despite medical belief that the plague was due to a corrupted atmosphere, people soon found that it could be passed on by contact with the sufferer. Boccaccio himself noticed the dangers of infection: "The virulence of the pest was the greater by reason that intercourse was apt to convey it from the sick to the whole, just as fire devours things dry or greasy when they are brought close to it. Nay, the evil went yet further, for not merely by speech or association with the

*The dangers of infection*

sick was the malady communicated to the healthy with consequent peril of common death; but any that touched the clothes of the sick or aught else that had been touched or used by them, seemed thereby to contract the disease (20)."

The rapidity with which the disease spread from person to

Italian merchants on a voyage to buy goods from the Middle East

Giovanni Boccaccio (*c.* 1313–75), the Italian author, who wrote a vivid eye-witness account of the plague in Florence

person in so many different ways was the most frightening aspect of the visitation. One chronicler wrote: "The contagious nature of the disease is indeed the most terrible of all the terrors, for when anyone who is infected by it dies, all who see him in his sickness, or visit him, or do any business with him, or even carry him to the grave, quickly follow him thither, and there is no known means of protection (21)."

*Indiscriminate death*

To the medieval mind, it was very disturbing to find that, if the Black Death were God's punishment for wickedness, it claimed its victims without discrimination—good and bad, Christian and heathen. Knighton told a story which showed this outlook: "The King of Tharsis, seeing so sudden and unheard of a mortality among his subjects, set out with a great multitude of nobles towards Avignon to the Pope . . . He purposed to be baptized a Christian, believing that God's vengeance had fallen upon his people by reason of their evil lack of faith. But, after twenty days' journey, hearing that the plague wrought as great havoc among Christians as among other nations, he turned and went no farther on that way, but hastened home unto his own country (22)."

No amount of prayers and penance could seem to stem the plague in its advance towards Europe. The very foundations of medieval society were soon to be shaken. People prepared for death.

27

# 3 The Black Death in Europe

IN THE 1300s, Florence was one of Europe's greatest cities. It was the first to experience a violent and widespread outbreak of the Black Death. What this meant for the people of a large town can be imagined from Boccaccio's well-known eyewitness account: "In Florence, despite all that human wisdom and forethought could devise to avert it, as the cleansing of the city from many impurities by officials appointed for the purpose, the refusal of entrance to all sick folk, and the adoption of many precautions for the preservation of health; despite also humble supplications addressed to God, and often repeated both in public procession and otherwise, by the devout; towards the beginning of the spring of the said year the doleful effects of the pestilence began to be horribly apparent by symptoms that shewed as if miraculous . . .

"Which maladies seemed to set entirely at naught both the art of the physician, and the virtues of the physic. Indeed, whether it was that the disorder [defied] such treatment, or that the physicians were at fault— besides the qualified there was now a multitude . . . who practised without having received the slightest tincture of medical science . . . in either case . . . almost all . . . died, and in most cases without any fever or other attendant malady . . . (23)"

People reacted differently to the coming of the plague: "Divers apprehensions and imaginations were engendered in the minds of such as were left alive; inclining almost all of them to the same harsh resolution; to wit, to shun and abhor all contact with the sick and all that belonged to them, thinking thereby to make each his own health secure . . .

"There were those who thought that to live temperately and avoid

*Plague in Florence*

*Human reactions*

29

*Opposite* A monk dies during a procession calling upon God to end the plague

Some richer people tried to live secluded lives to avoid contact with plague carriers

all excess would count for much as a preservative against seizures of this kind. Wherefore, they banded together, and, disassociating themselves from all others, formed communities in houses where there were no sick. [They] lived a separate and secluded life, which they regulated with the utmost care, avoiding every kind of luxury, but eating and drinking very moderately of the most delicate viands and the finest wines, holding converse with none but one another, lest tidings of sickness or death should reach them, and diverting their minds with music and such other delights as they could devise.

*Opposite* For others, the Black Death was a time of merriment—"Eat, drink and be merry, for tomorrow we may die"

"Others . . . maintained that to drink freely, to frequent places of public resort, and to take their pleasure with song and revel . . . was the sovereign remedy for so great an evil. And that which they affirmed they also put into practice, so far as they were able, resorting day and night now to this tavern, now to that, drinking with an entire disregard of rule or measure, and by preference making the houses of others, as it were, their inns . . . The owners, seeing death imminent, had become as reckless of their property as of their lives; so that most of the houses were open to all comers, and no distinction observed between the stranger who presented himself and the rightful lord . . .

"In this extremity of our city's sufferings and tribulation the venerable authority of laws, human and divine, was abused and all but totally dissolved, for lack of those who should have administered and enforced them, most of whom, like the rest of the citizens, were either dead or sick or so hard beset for servants that they were unable to execute any office; whereby every man was free to do what was right in his own eyes (24)."

*Precautions or flight?* Some tried to ward off the infection; others fled the city. Others "kept a middle course between them . . . living with a degree of freedom sufficient to satisfy their appetites, and not as recluses. They therefore walked abroad, carrying in their hands flowers or fragrant herbs or divers sorts of spices, which they frequently raised to their noses, deeming it an excellent thing thus to comfort the brain with such perfumes, because the air seemed to be everywhere laden and reeking with the stench emitted by the dead and dying, and the odours of drugs.

"Some again, the most sound, perhaps in judgement, as they were also the most harsh in temper, affirmed that there was no medicine for the disease superior or equal in efficiency to flight . . . A multitude of men and women, negligent of all but themselves, deserted their city, their houses, their estates, their kinsfolk, their goods, and went into voluntary exile, or migrated to the country, as if God, in visiting men with this pestilence in requital of their iniquities, would not pursue them with His wrath wherever they might be, but intended the destruction of such alone as remained within the circuit of the walls of the city . . . (25)"

*City of fear* People avoided each other as never before: "Tedious were it to recount how citizen avoided citizen, how among neighbours was scarce found any that showed fellow-feeling for another, how kinsfolk held aloof and never met, or but rarely. Enough that this sore affliction entered so deep into the minds of men and women that, in the horror thereof, brother was forsaken by brother, nephew by uncle, brother by sister and, oftentimes, husband by wife. Nay . . . fathers and mothers were found to abandon their own children, untended, unvisited, to their fate, as if they had been strangers . . .

"In consequence of which dearth of servants, and dereliction of the sick . . . it came to pass . . . that no woman, however dainty, fair or well-born, shrank, when stricken by the disease, from the ministrations of a man . . . or scrupled to expose to him every part of her body, with no more shame than if he had been a woman, submitting of necessity to that which her malady required. Wherefrom, perchance, there resulted in after-time some loss of modesty in such as recovered . . . (26)"

The dead were hurried to the grave without ceremony "It had been . . . the custom for the women that were neighbours or of kin to the deceased to gather in his house with the women that were most closely connected with him, to wail with them in common, while on the other hand his male kinsfolk and neighbours . . . assembled without, in front of the house, to receive the corpse; and so the dead man was borne on the shoulders of his peers, with funeral pomp of taper and dirge, to the church selected by him before his death. *Hurried funerals*

"These rites, as the pestilence waxed in fury, were either in whole or in great part disused and gave way to others of a novel order. For not only did no crowd of women surround the bed of the dying, but many passed from this life unregarded, and few indeed were they to whom were accorded the lamentations and bitter tears of sorrowing relations. Nay, for the most part, their place was taken by the laugh, the jest, the festal gathering; observances which the women—domestic piety in large measure set aside—had adopted with very great advantage to their health.

"Few also there were whose bodies were attended to the church by more than ten or twelve neighbours, and those not the honourable and respected citizens, but a sort of corpse-carrier drawn from the

33

The spread of the Black Death made funerals rare as people were so afraid
of catching the disease

baser ranks, who called themselves *becchini* and performed such
offices for hire, would shoulder the bier and, with hurried steps,
carry it, not to the church of the dead man's choice, but to that
which was nearest at hand, with four or six priests in front and a
candle or two, or, perhaps none. Nor did the priests distress

themselves with too long and solemn an office, but with the aid of the *becchini* hastily consigned the corpse to the first tomb which they found untenanted . . .

"Many died daily or nightly in the public streets. Of many others, who died at home, the departure was hardly observed by their neighbours, until the stench of their putrefying bodies carried the tidings; and what with their corpses and the corpses of others who died on every hand the whole place was a sepulchre (27)."

As the deaths increased, funerals became even more perfunctory: "It was the common practice of most of the neighbours, moved no less by fear of contamination by the putrefying bodies than by charity towards the deceased, to drag the corpses out of the houses with their own hands, aided, perhaps, by a porter—if a porter was to be had—and to lay them round in front of the doors, where any one that made the round might have seen, especially in the morning,

*Indifference to the dead*

Plague victims at Tournai are hurriedly buried in pits

more of them than he could count.

"Afterwards they would have biers brought up or, in default, planks whereon they laid them. Nor was it only once or twice that one and the same bier carried two or three corpses, at once; but [many] such cases occurred, one bier sufficing for husband and wife, two or three brothers, father and son, and so forth. And times without number it happened that, as two priests bearing the cross were on their way to perform the last office for some one, three or four biers were brought up by the porters in rear of them. So that, whereas the priests supposed that they had but one corpse to bury, they discovered that there were six or eight, or sometimes more. Nor were their obsequies honoured by either tears, or lights, or crowds of mourners . . . A dead man was then of no more account than a dead goat would be today . . . (28)"

Death around the city

The plague began to ravage the countryside around Florence: "As consecrated ground there was not in extent sufficient to provide tombs for the vast multitude of corpses . . . they dug for each grave-yard, as soon as it was full, a huge trench in which they laid the corpses as they arrived by hundreds at a time, piling them up as merchandise is stowed in the hold of a ship, tier upon tier, each covered with a little earth, until the trench would hold no more.

"But I spare to rehearse with minute particularity each of the woes that came upon our city, and say in brief that, harsh as was the tenor of her fortunes, the surrounding country knew no mitigation; for there . . . in sequestered villages, or on the open champaign [countryside], by the wayside, on the farm, in the home-stead; the poor, hapless husbandmen and their families, forlorn of physician's care or servants' tendance, perished day and night alike, not as men but rather as beasts.

"They too, like the citizens, abandoned all rule of life, all habit of industry, all counsel of prudence. Nay, one and all, as if expecting each day to be their last, not merely ceased to aid Nature to yield her fruit in due season . . . but left no means unused, which in-genuity could devise, to waste their accumulated store; denying shelter to their oxen, asses, sheep, goats, pigs, fowls, nay even to their dogs, man's most faithful companions, and driving them out into the fields to roam at large amid the unsheaved, nay unreaped corn . . . (29)"

Death rode as triumphantly over nobles and churchmen as the poor

When at last the plague had passed, Boccaccio dwelt upon the losses the city had suffered: "Between March and the ensuing July, upwards of a hundred thousand human beings lost their lives within the walls of the city of Florence, which before the deadly visitation would not have been supposed to contain so many people!

*Sorrowful aftermath*

37

Religious fanatics called the Flagellants tried to prevent the plague by self-punishment

"How many grand palaces, how many stately homes, how many splendid residences, once full of retainers, of lords, of ladies, were now left desolate of all, even to the meanest servant! How many families of historic fame, of vast ancestral domains and wealth proverbial, found now no scion to continue the succession! How many brave men, how many fair ladies, how many gallant youths, whom any physician, were he Galen, Hippocrates or Aesculapius himself, would have pronounced in the soundest of health, broke fast with their kinsfolk, comrades and friends in the morning, and when evening came, supped with their forefathers in the other world! (30)"

*Burial pits*    As the plague spread, other Italian cities suffered in the same way. Agnolo di Tura wrote of Siena: "Father abandoned child, wife, husband; one brother, another, for this illness seemed to strike through the breath and the sight. And so they died. And no one could be found to bury the dead for money or for friendship . . . And in many places in Siena great pits were dug and piled deep with huge heaps of the dead . . . And I, Agnolo di Tura, called the Fat, buried my five children with my own hands, and so did many others likewise. And there were also many dead throughout the city who were so sparsely covered with earth that the dogs dragged them forth and devoured their bodies (31)."

The Black Death reached France within a few months of the *Brave nuns* first outbreak on the Italian mainland. It raged throughout the winter of 1348-9 in Paris. There, a community of nuns showed bravery that set them apart from most people who wished to flee the capital: "There was so great a mortality among people of both sexes, of the young rather than of the old, that it was hardly possible to bury them. In the Hôtel-Dieu at Paris, so great was the mortality that for a long time more than five hundred corpses were carted daily to the churchyard of St. Innocent to be buried. And those holy sisters, having no fear of death, tended the sick with all sweetness and humility, putting all honour behind their back. The greater number of these sisters, many times renewed by death, now rest in peace with Christ, as we must piously believe (32)."

Smaller French towns, too, suffered badly. One was St. Marie *Sudden death* Laumont in Normandy; as late as June, 1349, the King authorized the Mayor to open a new cemetery because "the mortality . . . is so marvellously great that people are dying there suddenly, as quickly as between one evening and the following morning and often quicker than that (33)."

As the plague spread into Germany and other countries, there *Flagellants* appeared religious fanatics, known as Flagellants; these whipped themselves in frenzy to avert God's wrath: "Amongst them, many of both sexes were barefooted, some were in sack cloth, some covered with ashes, wailing as they walked, tearing their hair, and lashing themselves with scourges even to the point where blood was drawn (34)."

But still the plague spread. Very soon it was to be carried even further north, over the Channel, and into southern England.

# 4 England Infected

ROBERT OF AVESBURY said the Black Death first reached England _The plague's arrival_ on the Dorset coast in August, 1348: "It began in England, in the neighbourhood of Dorchester, about the Feast of St. Peter ad Vinculas, 1348, immediately spreading rapidly from place to place, and many persons who were healthy in the early morning, before midday were snatched from human affairs. It permitted none whom it marked down to live more than three or four days, without choice of persons, save only in the case of a few rich people. On the same day of their death, the bodies of twenty, forty, sixty, and many times more persons were delivered to the Church's burial in the same pit (35)."

The Chronicle of the Greyfriars at Lynn was more explicit and _Death ships_ put the start of the plague earlier, in June: "In this year 1348, in Melcombe, in the county of Dorset, a little before the Feast of St. John the Baptist [24th June], two ships, one of them from Bristol, came alongside. One of the sailors had brought with him from Gascony the seeds of the terrible pestilence and, through him, the men of that town of Melcombe were the first in England to be infected (36)."

The ship may have sailed from the Channel Islands. The plague _Channel_ was already raging there so violently that King Edward III wrote _Islands_ to the Governor of Jersey: "By reason of the mortality among the people and fishing folk of these islands, which here as elsewhere has been so great, our rent for the fishing which has been yearly paid us, cannot be now obtained without the impoverishing and excessive oppression of those fishermen still left (37)." _Southampton_

According to Knighton, the two great ports of Southampton and _and Bristol_

_Opposite_ Much of our knowledge of the Black Death in England comes from histories and chronicles written at the time

Bristol were soon struck by the plague, which travelled perhaps by both land and water: "Then the dreadful pestilence made its way through the coast land by Southampton, and reached Bristol, and there perished almost the whole strength of the town, as it were surprised by sudden death; for few kept their beds more than two or three days, or even half a day. Then this cruel death spread on all sides, following the course of the sun (38)."

*All over the kingdom*    From the south coast Geoffrey le Baker recorded, the plague spread eastwards into the rest of the kingdom. It "deprived first the sea ports in Dorset, and then the whole district of almost all their inhabitants, and spreading thence it raged so violently throughout Devon and Somerset as far as Bristol that the people of Gloucester would not let those of Bristol come into their parts, for they all thought that the breath of persons who lived among those who

A sailor, landing at Bristol from France, brought the plague to England

were thus dying was infected. But at length it invaded Gloucester, yea Oxford, London, and at last the whole of England, with such violence that scarcely one person in ten of either sex survived (39)."

So began the terrible year of 1349. As a chronicler grimly remembered, hardly any town or village was unaffected. Between a quarter and a third of the people died from the Black Death in England: "Of which twenty-second year and the next of the King's reign is little to be written, nothing being done abroad, in effect, through the great mortality of the plague that raged all over the land; which as the historiographers of that time deliver, consumed nine parts in ten of the men through England, scarce leaving a tenth man alive (40)."

In January, 1349, Ralph of Shrewsbury, Bishop of Bath and Wells, wrote to all the priests in his diocese. His letter reveals vividly the devastation already caused by the plague in Somerset: "The contagious pestilence of the present day, which is spreading far and wide, has left many parish churches and other livings in our diocese without parson or priest to care for their parishioners. Since no priests can be found who are willing . . . to take on the pastoral care of these aforesaid places, nor to visit the sick and administer to them the Sacraments of the Church (perhaps for fear of infection and contagion), we understand that many people are dying without the Sacrament of Penance. These people have no idea what resources are open to them in such a case of need and believe that, whatever the straits they may be in, no confession of their sins is useful or meritorious unless it is made to a duly ordained priest.

"We therefore, [wish] to provide for the salvation of souls and to bring back from their paths of error those who have wandered [and] do strictly enjoin and command . . . the rectors, vicars and parish priests in all your churches, and you, the deans elsewhere in your deaneries where the comfort of a priest is denied the people, that . . . you should at once publicly command and persuade all men . . . that, if they are on the point of death and cannot secure the services of a priest, then they should make confession to each other . . . whether to a layman or, if no man is present, then even to a woman.

"We urge you, by these present letters, in the bowels of Jesus Christ, to do this . . . And, in case anyone might fear that a lay confessor would make public the confessions which they heard

43

Cy cōmence le oroison.
E te salue tres saint et
tres precieux corps de mō
createur ihucrist et qui es

and, for this reason, might hesitate to confess himself to such a person even in time of need, you should announce to all . . . who might hear confessions in this way, that they are bound by the laws of the Church to conceal and keep secret such confessions, and that they are prohibited by sacred canonical decrees from betraying such confessions by word, sign, or any other means, except at the wish of those who have made such confession. If they break this law then they should know that they commit a most grievous sin and, in so doing, incur the wrath of Almighty God and of the whole Church (41)."

The Bishop showed how serious he felt things were by greatly relaxing the usual rules of the medieval Church: "The Sacrament of the Eucharist, when no priest is available, may be administered by a deacon. If, however, there is no priest to adminster the Sacrament of Extreme Unction, then, as in other matters, faith must suffice (42)."

Further northward, Bishop Wulstan Bransford of Worcester had to forbid, for health reasons, all further burials in the cathedral churchyard. He opened a new graveyard in the city to receive the numerous dead: "The burials have in these days, to our sorrow, increased . . . (for the great number of the dead in our days has never been equalled); and, on this account, both for our brethren in the said church . . . for the citizens of the said city and others dwelling therein, and for all others coming to the place, because of the various dangers which may probably await them from the corruption of the bodies, we desire, as far as God shall grant us, to provide the best remedy (43)."

*Dead threaten the living*

By now the plague had reached London, the largest city in the land. It was also the dirtiest, despite efforts made to clean it, such as this proclamation issued by Edward II in 1309: "Seeing that the people in the town do cause the ordure that has been collected in their houses, to be carried and placed in the streets, and in the lanes of the City, whereas they ought to have it carried to the Thames, or elsewhere out of the town; and that thereby the streets and lanes are more encumbered than they used to be, we do forbid, on the King's behalf, that from henceforth any person shall have the ordure that has been collected in his house, carried into the King's highways; but let them cause the same to be

*London: a filthy city*

45

*Opposite* As the disease spread, fewer people attended church and many churches were left without priests

carried to the Thames, or elsewhere out of the City, whither it used to be carried.

"And if any one shall do so, he shall be amerced [fined], the first time, in forty pence, and afterwards, in half a mark each time; and nevertheless, he shall have the same removed at his own charges. And the same penalty shall be incurred by those before whose houses dung shall be found, if, after the dung has been placed there, they shall not immediately have their Alderman told by whom such dung has been so brought there. Also, no person shall have any dung raked or removed to the front of the houses of others (44)."

According to Robert of Avesbury, the Black Death raged in London from late autumn, 1348, to the early summer of 1349 (the Feast of All Saints is 1st November; Michaelmas is 29th September; Whitsunday in 1349 was 31st May): "Reaching London about the feast of All Saints, it slew many persons daily, and increased so greatly that from the feast of the Purification until just after Easter, in a newly-made cemetery in Smithfield the bodies of more than 200 persons, besides those that were buried in other cemeteries of the same city, were buried every day. But by the intervention of the Grace of the Holy Spirit, it ceased in London on Whitsunday, continuing to spread towards the north, in which parts it also ceased about Michaelmas, 1349 (45)."

*Death in the city*   About 30,000 out of a total population of some 70,000 died from the Black Death in London. Geoffrey le Baker described the sufferings of its people. The new cemeteries provided by Ralph Stratford, Bishop of London, and Sir Walter Manny, the soldier and courtier, were both at Smithfield, then an open space outside the City walls: "Since the cemeteries did not suffice, fields were chosen for burying the dead. The Bishop of London bought that croft in London called 'Nomannes lond', and the lord Walter Manny the one called 'the newe chierche hawe', where he founded a religious house for the burial of the dead. Suits in the King's Bench and Common pleas came of necessity to a standstill. A few noblemen died, among whom were the Lord John of Montgomery, Captain of Calais and the Lord Clisteles, who both died in Calais and were buried in London . . .

"But innumerable common people and a multitude of monks and other clerks known to God alone passed away. The pestilence

vnd gaifleten fich felber vil vnd vaft vnd vie =
len vnder auf peichten vnd abfoluierten felber
in ein ander vnd hielten vnd gepulen vil an
ein ander zo hielten hunderliche ding vn falfch
weifz vnd artиel vnder criften gelauben vnd

The Flagellants came to England in 1349, often performing their rituals in
front of St. Paul's Cathedral

seized especially the young and strong, commonly sparing the elderly and feeble. Scarcely any one ventured to touch the sick, and healthy persons shunned the once, and still, precious possessions of the dead, as infectious. People perfectly well on one day were found dead on the next.

"Some were tormented with abscesses in various parts of their body, and from these many, by means of lancing, or with long suffering, recovered. Others had small black pustules scattered over the whole surface of their body, from which very few, nay, scarcely a single person, returned to life and health. This great pestilence, which began at Bristol about the Feast of the Assumption [15th August], and at London about Michaelmas, raged in England for a whole year and more, so that many villages were utterly emptied of every human being (46)."

*Frenzy of Flagellants*      The Flagellants came to London when the plague was waning. Knighton told how they held their ceremonies on an open plot before St. Paul's Cathedral. But they were soon deported as undesirable aliens: "In the year 1349, about Michaelmas, more than six score men, natives, for the greater part, of Holland and Zeeland, came to London from Flanders. And twice a day, sometimes in the Church of St. Paul, sometimes in other places of the City, in sight of all the people, covered with a linen cloth from the thighs to the heels, the rest of the body being bare, and each wearing a cap marked before and behind with a red cross, and holding a scourge with three thongs having each a knot through which sharp points were fixed, went barefoot in procession one after another, scourging their bare and bleeding bodies.

"Four of them would sing in their own tongue, all the others making response, in the manner of litanies sung by Christians. Three times in their procession all together would fling themselves upon the ground, their hands outspread in the form of a cross, continually singing. And beginning with the last, one after another, as they lay, each in turn struck the man before him once with his flail; and so from one to another, each performed the same rite to the last. Then each resumed his usual garments, and still wearing their caps and holding their flails, they returned to their lodging. And it was said that they performed the same penance every evening (47)."

# 5 Prayer and Despair

THE BLACK DEATH spread both from London and the Channel ports across south-eastern England. William of Dene, a monk of Rochester, described the problems facing his bishop in administering the Church as it was decimated by death: "In this year, a plague of a kind which had never been met with before ravaged our land of England. The Bishop of Rochester, who maintained only a small household, lost four priests, five esquires, ten attendants, seven young clerics and six pages, so that nobody was left to serve him in any capacity. At Malling he consecrated two abbesses but both died almost immediately, leaving only four established nuns and four novices. One of these the Bishop put in the charge of the lay members and the other of the religious, for it proved impossible to find anyone suitable to act as abbess (48)." *Disruption*

William was dismayed by the desolation caused by the plague in the Kentish countryside, though his suggestion that a third of the land of the whole kingdom lay idle is an exaggeration: "To our great grief, the plague carried off so vast a multitude of people of both sexes that nobody could be found who would bear the corpses to the grave. Men and women carried their own children on their shoulders to the church and threw them into a common pit. From these pits such an appalling stench was given off that scarcely anyone dared even to walk beside the cemeteries. *Desolation in Kent*

"There was so marked a deficiency of labourers and workmen of every kind at this period that more than a third of the land in the whole realm was let lie idle. All the labourers, skilled or unskilled, were so carried away by the spirit of revolt that neither King, nor law, nor justice, could restrain them . . . (49)"

The plague caused a serious shortage of people in the monasteries and Church

Haymo de Hythe, who had been Bishop of Rochester since 1319, survived the Black Death, but his household died all around him: "During the whole of that winter and the following spring, the Bishop of Rochester, aged and infirm, remained at Trottiscliffe [his country manor between Sevenoaks and Rochester], bewailing the terrible changes which had overcome the world. In every manor of his diocese buildings were falling into decay and there was hardly one manor which returned as much as £100. In the monastery of Rochester supplies ran short and the brethren had great difficulty in getting enough to eat; to such a point that the monks were obliged either to grind their own bread or to go without. The prior, however, ate everything of the best (50)."

*Parliament prorogued*     The summoning of Parliament was twice postponed in 1349. The reasons were given in this writ issued to sheriffs and others summoned to attend at Westminster on 10th March: "Whereas lately, by reason of the deadly pestilence then prevailing, we caused the Parliament that was summoned to meet at Westminster on the Monday after the Feast of St. Hilary [13th January] to be prorogued until the quinzaine of Easter next—and because the aforesaid pestilence is increasing with more than its usual severity, in Westminster and in the City of London and the surrounding districts, whereby the coming of the magnates and other our faithful lieges to that place at this time, would probably be too dangerous—for

As the peasants died the fields became neglected and food was often scarce

51

Although monks led secluded lives, they were not spared from the plague
St. Alban's monastery soon lost forty monks

this, and for certain other obvious reasons, we have thought fit to postpone the said Parliament until we shall issue further summons (51)."

North of London, the plague was at its worst in Hertfordshire *An abbot dies* during the spring of 1349. St. Albans Abbey suffered badly; its Abbot, Michael de Mentmore, was one of the first to die. The Abbey's records tell us: "Being the first to suffer from the dread disease which was later to carry off his monks. He began to feel the first symptoms on Maundy Thursday, but out of reverence for the festival and remembering our Lord's humility, he celebrated High Mass and then, before taking his dinner, humbly and devoutly washed the feet of the poor. After he had taken his dinner he proceeded to wash and kiss the feet of all the brethren and to carry out all the offices of the day alone and without assistance. The next day when his sickness became worse, he took to his bed and, as a true Catholic, made his confession with a contrite heart and received the sacrament of extreme unction. Amidst the sorrow of all who surrounded him he endured until noon on Easter Day . . . And there died at that time forty-seven monks . . . (52)"

The *Chronicon Angliae* by Thomas of Walsingham, a monk who *Monasteries* also was at St. Albans, spoke of the especially high losses inside the monasteries. The plague often spread rapidly there, as might be expected in communities of men living closely together: "A great mortality spread throughout the world, starting from the northern and western regions, and raging with such great slaughter that scarcely the half of mankind survived. And towns that were formerly very thickly populated were left destitute of inhabitants, the plague being so violent that the living were scarce able to bury the dead. For in some religious houses, of twenty monks, scarce two survived. For, to say nothing of other monasteries, in the monastery of St. Albans more than forty monks died in a short space of time. And it was estimated that scarcely a tenth part of the people had been left alive. The pestilence was immediately followed by a murrain [epidemic] among beasts. At that time, revenues wasted away, and for want of husbandmen, who were nowhere to be found, lands remained uncultivated. And such misery followed these misfortunes that the world never afterwards had the opportunity of returning to its former condition (53)."

53

*Overleaf* The small, crowded, dirty medieval towns were an ideal breeding ground for the plague

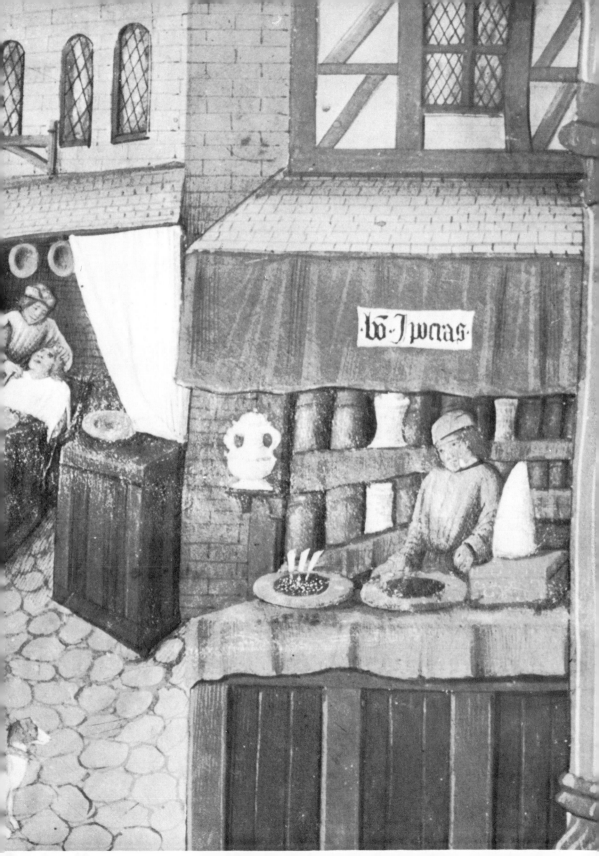

The common clerk of Grimsby in Lincolnshire told how the Black Death raged for over a year in the great diocese of Lincoln, which then stretched from the River Humber to the River Thames: "In 1349 there was that great pestilence in Lincoln which spread all over parts of the world, beginning on Palm Sunday [16th April] in the year aforesaid and enduring until the feast of the Nativity of St. John the Baptist next following [24th June], when it ceased, God be praised who reigns for ever and ever, Amen (54)."

The terror of the plague was increased because medieval people had no idea of statistics, and exaggerated its toll. Thus, Knighton wrote of heavy deaths in Leicester, but since the town probably had only 3,000 inhabitants, his numbers must be too large: "And there died at Leicester, in the small parish of St. Leonard more than 380 persons, in the parish of Holy Cross, 400, in the parish of St. Margaret's, Leicester, 700; and so in every parish, in a great multitude (55)."

John Gynwell, Bishop of Lincoln, tried to protect both religion and trade by making emergency provisions for the absolution of sinners and the recovery of debts: "The Bishop of Lincoln sent notice throughout his whole diocese giving general power to all priests, as well regulars as seculars, of hearing confessions and giving absolution to all persons with full episcopal authority, except only in case of debt. And in this case, the debtor was to pay the debt, if he were able, while he lived, or others were to be appointed to do so from his property after his death. In the same way the Pope gave plenary [full] remission of all offences to all receiving absolution at the point of death, and granted that this power should endure until Easter next following, and that every one might choose his own confessor at will (56)."

Further north, William de la Zouche, Archbishop of York, issued a call to repentance. Two years earlier he had led the English army to victory against the Scots in the Battle of Neville's Cross, and his call to repentance began in a typically martial strain: "In so far as the life of men upon earth is warfare, it is no wonder that those who battle amidst the wickedness of the world are sometimes disturbed by uncertain events; on one occasion favourable, on another adverse. For almighty God sometimes allows those whom he loves to be chastened so that their strength can be made complete

The Scots hoped to attack the plague-ridden English army, but were themselves struck by the disease

by the outpouring of spiritual grace in their time of infirmity. Everybody knows, since the news is now widely spread, what great pestilence, mortality and infection of the air there are in divers parts of the world and which, at this moment, are threatening in particular the land of England. This, surely, must be caused by the sins of men who, made complacent by their prosperity, forget the bounty of the most high Giver (57)."

As the Black Death overtook the north of England, the Scots decided to avenge themselves on the English for their recent defeat. But their army was itself struck by the plague: "The Scots, hearing of the dreadful pestilence in England, surmised that it had come about at the hand of an avenging God, and it became an oath among them, so that, according to the common report, they were accustomed to swear 'be the foul death of England'. Thus, believing that a terrible vengeance of God had overtaken the English, they came together in Selkirk forest with the intention of invading the realm of England, when the fierce mortality overtook them and their ranks were thinned by sudden and terrible death, so that in a short time some 5,000 perished. And as the rest, the strong and the feeble, were making ready to return to their own country, they were pursued and surprised by the English, who killed a very great number of them (58)."

Carried partly by the fleeing Scottish soldiers, the Black Death moved remorsely across the River Tweed with results described by

*Scots restive*

57

John of Fordun: "In the year 1350, there was, in the kingdom of Scotland, so great a pestilence and plague among men . . . as, from the beginning of the world even unto modern times, had never been heard of by man, nor is found in books, for the enlightenment of those who come after. For, to such a pitch did that plague wreak its cruel spite, that nearly a third of mankind were thereby made to pay the debt of nature.

"Moreover, by God's will, this evil led to a strange and unwonted kind of death, insomuch that the flesh of the sick was somehow puffed out and swollen, and they dragged out their earthly life for barely two days. Now this everywhere attacked especially the meaner sort and common people—seldom the magnates. Men shrank from it so much that, through fear of contagion, sons, fleeing as from the face of leprosy or from an adder, durst not go and see their parents in the throes of death (59)."

By the end of 1350 there was scarcely anywhere in Britain that had remained untouched by the plague. Families were broken; communities shattered. English society itself had been shaken to its very foundations.

# 6 A Changed Society

*Disillusion*

MATTEO VILLANI, a Florentine historian, wrote of the disillusionment that filled the survivors of the Black Death: "Those few discreet folk who remained alive expected many things, all of which, by reason of the corruption of sin, failed among mankind, whose minds followed marvellously in the contrary direction. They believed that those whom God's grace had saved from death, having beheld the destruction of their neighbours . . . would become better-conditioned, humble, virtuous and Catholic; that they would guard themselves from iniquity and sin and would be full of love and charity towards one another.

"But no sooner had the plague ceased than we saw the contrary. For since men were few and since, by hereditary succession, they abounded in earthly goods, they forgot the past as though it had never been, and gave themselves up to a more shameful and disordered life than they had led before. For, mouldering in ease, they dissolutely abandoned themselves to the sin of gluttony, with feasts and taverns and delight of delicate viands; and again to games of hazard and to unbridled lechery, inventing strange and unaccustomed fashions and indecent manners in their garments . . . (60)"

*Quarrels and riots*

As Villani came to realize, the plague and its effects led most people to display, not their best, but rather their worst qualities. This was true in all the countries which had suffered: "Men thought that, by reason of the fewness of mankind, there should be abundance of all produce of the land. Yet, on the contrary, by reason of men's ingratitude, everything came to unwonted scarcity and remained long thus; nay, in certain countries . . . there were grievous and unwonted famines. Again, men dreamed of wealth and

59

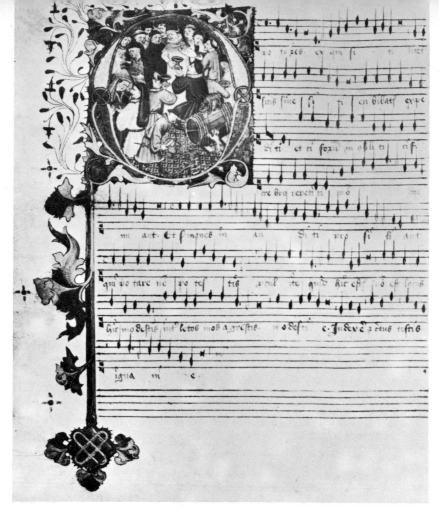

People complained that peasants who had survived the Black Death had forgotten how to work

abundance in garments . . . yet, in fact, things turned out widely different, for most commodities were more costly, by twice or more, than before the plague. And the price of labour and the work of all trades and crafts rose in disorderly fashion beyond the double. Law-suits and disputes and quarrels and riots rose elsewhere among citizens in every land . . . (61)"

In England an immediate effect of the Black Death was a breakdown of law and order. People took advantage of the confusion and distress to rob the survivors and pillage the homes of the victims. In the village of Rewe, in Wales, two brothers, Madoc and Kenwric

Ap Ririd "came by night in the Pestilence to the house of Aylmar after the death of the wife of Aylmar and took from the same house one water pitcher and basin, value one shilling, old iron, value fourpence. And they also present that Madoc and Kenwric came by night to the house of Almar in the village of Rewe in the Pestilence, and from that house stole three oxen of John le Parker and three cows, value six shillings (62)."

William of Dene was worried, too, by the spirit of revolt among the labourers and the selfishness displayed by the clergy: "The people for the greater part ever became more depraved, more prone to every vice and more inclined than before to evil and wickedness, not thinking of death nor of the past plague nor of their own salvation . . . Priests, little weighing the sacrifice of a contrite spirit, betook themselves to where they could get larger stipends than in their own benefices, on which account many benefices remained unserved. Day by day, the dangers to soul both in clergy and people multiplied . . . The labourers and skilled workmen were imbued with such a spirit of rebellion that neither king, law nor justice could curb them (63)."

The Church of England had suffered heavy losses among its clergy. John Stratford, Archbishop of Canterbury, died in August, 1348. His successor, John Offord, died in May, 1349, before even being enthroned. He was followed by Thomas Bradwardine, who died the following August. Many priests had died, too, and Knighton spoke disparagingly of the middle-aged widowers who were ordained to take their places: "There was everywhere so great a scarcity of priests that many churches were left destitute, without divine service, masses, matins, vespers or sacraments. A chaplain was scarcely to be had to serve any church for less than £10 or 10 marks, and whereas when there was an abundance of priests before the pestilence a chaplain could be had for 4, 5 or 11 marks, with his board, at this time there was scarcely one willing to accept any vicarage at £20 or 20 marks. Within a little time, however, vast numbers of men whose wives had died in the pestilence flocked to take orders, many of whom were illiterate, and as it were mere laymen, save so far as they could read a little, although without understanding (64)." (A mark was worth two-thirds of £1).

William Langland, in his poem *The Vision of Piers Plowman*,

*Problems of the Church*

61

gives a vivid picture of contemporary life. He condemned those clergy who left their parishes and committed the sin of simony by buying better posts as priests who sang masses in London (65):

> Parsons and parish priests pleynëd [complained] them to the bishop,
> That their parishes were poor sith [since] the pestilence-time,
>> To have a licence and a leave at London for to dwell,
>> And singen there for simony; for silver is sweet.

*Archbishop's decree*    In an attempt to stop this abuse, the Archbishop of Canterbury decreed that priests must serve their own churches and receive moderate payment: "The general complaint reaches us, and that effective teacher, experience, shows us, that the priests now surviving, not considering that they have been preserved from the perils of the late pestilence to perform their ministry for the sake of God's people . . . not caring to undertake such cure, or bear the burdens pertaining to it, and betake themselves to the celebration of annuals and other private masses.

"And, not contented with the accustomed stipends, they exact excessive payment for their services, so that under an unpretentious name, and with but light labour, they may claim more profit than if they had cure of souls . . . It will come to pass, unless their unreasonable appetite be restrained, that many churches . . . will remain utterly destitute of the services of priests (66)."

*Change in education*    As most teachers were clerics, the deaths among the clergy brought about a far-reaching change in English education. Until then, as John Trevisa explained, school children were taught in Norman French: "Children in school, against the usage and manner of all other nations, are compelled to leave their own language, and to learn their lessons and their things in French, and so they have since the Normans came first into England. Also, gentlemen's children are taught to speak French from the time that they are rocked in their cradle, and can speak and play with a child's brooch. And uplandish men will liken themselves to gentlemen, and try easily to speak French (67)."

Now, there were so few teachers who could teach French that English was studied in its place. This change was pioneered by John Cornwall, a grammar school master: "This manner was much used . . . For John Cornwall, a master of grammar, changed the

Children were taught in English at school since so many French-speaking
teachers had died

custom in grammar school, and construction of French into English;
and Richard Pencriche learned from him how to teach it to other
men of Pencriche, so that now in the year of our Lord 1385 . . .
in all the grammar schools of England, children leave French and
construe and learn in English.

"And they have thereby an advantage on one side, and a disadvantage on the other. Their advantage is that they learn their
grammar in less time than children once did; the disadvantage is

that now children of grammar schools no more understand French than their left heel, and that is harmful for them if they should cross the sea and work in strange lands and in many other places. Also, gentlemen have now much to do to teach their children French (68)."

An important outcome was an Act of Parliament in 1362 ordering the law courts to use English instead of French: "It is often shown to the King by the prelates, dukes, earls, barons, and all the commons, what great mischiefs have happened to many persons, because the laws, customs, and statutes of the realm are not commonly known, by reason that they are pleaded, set forth and judged in the French tongue, which is too unknown in the said realm. So that people who plead or are impleaded in the King's courts and others, have no knowledge or understanding of what is said for or against them by their sergeants or pleaders . . .

"The said laws and customs would the sooner be learned and known, and better understood in the tongue used in this realm, and so everyone could better conduct himself without breaking the law, and better safeguard his inheritance and possessions. And in various other regions and countries where the King and the nobles and others of this kingdom have been, there is good governance and full right is done to all men, because their laws and customs are learned and used in the tongue of the land . . .

"For the above causes the King has ordained and established that all pleas which shall be pleaded in any of his courts before any of his justices . . . or before any other of his ministers, or in the courts and places of other lords of the realm, shall be shown, pleaded, defended, answered and debated in the English tongue . . . And they shall be entered and enrolled in Latin (69)."

*Universities* To the universities the Black Death brought gains; the great shortage of learned men led to the foundation of new colleges to train new scholars. Simon Islip, Archbishop of Canterbury, explained why he founded Canterbury College at Oxford: "Those who are truly learned and accomplished in every kind of learning have been largely exterminated in the epidemics, and that, because of the lack of opportunity, very few are coming forward at present to carry on such studies . . . (70)"

*Depopulation* In the countryside, depopulation caused long-lasting problems. In 1352 the patrons of two local churches at Great Colington and

New colleges were founded at universities to help train the scholars needed
to replace those who had died

TBD—3**

Little Colington jointly petitioned the Bishop of Hereford to unite their parishes: "The sore calamity of pestilence of men lately passed, which ravaged the whole world in every part, has so reduced the number of the people of the said churches and for that said reason there followed, and still exists, such a paucity of labourers and other inhabitants, such manifest sterility of the lands, and such notorious poverty in the said parishes, that the parishioners and receipts of both churches scarcely suffice to support one priest (71)."

Knighton told what this shortage of labour meant in the farms and fields: "In the same year there was a great murrain of sheep everywhere in the kingdom, so that in one place more than 5000 sheep died in a single pasture; and they rotted so that neither bird nor beast would approach them. There was great cheapness of all things, owing to the general fear of death, since very few people took any account of riches or property of any kind. A horse that was formerly worth forty shillings could be had for half a mark, a fat ox for four shillings, a cow for twelve pence, a heifer for six pence, a fat wether for four pence, a sheep for three pence, a lamb for two pence, a large pig for five pence; a stone of wool was worth nine pence.

"Sheep and oxen strayed at large through the fields and among the crops, and there were none to drive them off or herd them, but they perished in remote byways and hedges in inestimable numbers ... There was such great scarcity of servants that none knew what to do. For there was no recollection of such great and terrible mortality since the time of Vortigern, King of the Britons, in whose day, as Bede testifies, the living did not suffice to bury the dead (72)."

*Rotting crops*   When harvest-time came, even higher wages could not produce enough men to gather in the crops: "In the following autumn a reaper was not to be had for less than eight pence, with his food, a mower for less than ten pence, with food. Wherefore many crops rotted in the fields for want of men to gather them. But in the year of the pestilence, as has been said above, of other things, there was so great an abundance of all kinds of corn that they were scarcely regarded (73)."

*Landowners'*   Landlords began competing for tenants and labourers, and had
*problems*   to offer better terms than before: "After the pestilence many

buildings both great and small in all cities, towns, and boroughs
fell into ruins for want of inhabitants . . . In the same way many
villages and hamlets were depopulated, and there were no houses
left in them, all who had lived therein being dead . . . It seemed
likely that many such hamlets would never again be inhabited.
In the following winter there was such dearth of servants for all
sorts of labour as it was believed had never been before. For the
sheep and cattle strayed in all directions without herdsmen, and
all things were left with none to care for them.

"Thus necessaries became so dear that what had previously
been worth one penny was now worth four pence or five pence.
Moreover the great men of the land and other lesser lords who had
tenants, remitted the payment of their rents, lest the tenants should
go away, on account of the scarcity of servants and the high price of
all things—some half their rents, some more, some less, some for
one, two, or three years according as they could come to an agreement with them.

A tenant paying his rent

67

"Similarly, those who had let lands on labour-rents to tenants as is the custom in the case of villeins, were obliged to relieve and remit these services, either excusing them entirely, or taking them on easier terms, in the form of a small rent, lest their houses should be irreparably ruined and the land should remain uncultivated. And all sorts of food became excessively dear (74)."

*Threatening tenants* A note on the Court Roll of the manor of Rudheath shows how a landlord had to yield to his tenants if they threatened to go elsewhere: "In money remitted to the tenants . . . by the Justices of Chester and others, by the advice of the Lord, for the third part of their rent by reason of the plague which had been raging, because the tenants there wished to depart and leave the holdings on the Lord's hands unless they obtained this remission until the world do come better again, and the holdings possess a greater value: £10 13s 11¾d (75)."

When taking new tenants, it became common for a landlord to agree a lower rent until he could find a tenant willing to pay more. The Prior of Durham, for example, had to do this: "1366. Burdon. One messuage and three oxgangs of land, which had been Nicholas Ben's, are assigned to William Smyth, John of Heswell and Robert Dines, to have and to hold until another tenants who shall be willing to take the land and pay the old rent, viz. forty shillings per annum; the payment to be given at Whitsuntide under pain of loss of all the land which they hold from my lord prior. And be it known that they shall pay, for the first three years, by his grace, thirty shillings per annum (76)."

*An abbot's agreement* Another arrangement was to charge tenants a higher rent, but remit some of their feudal services. The Abbot of Eynsham in Oxfordshire did this on his manor of Woodeaton: "In the days of that mortality or pestilence which was in the year of our Lord 1349, there scarce remained two tenants on this manor, and these would have departed unless brother Nicholas of Upton, who was then abbot of the said manor, had made a new composition with them and with other tenants who came in.

"He agreed with them in the following form; namely that the said Walter and other tenants should be subject to certain dues; relief, heriot, merchet, and a certain amount of forced labour and that he should also pay a yearly rent of 13s 4d so long as it may please my

68

lord abbot; and may it please my lord to perpetuity, for the aforesaid services from which he is now released were not worth so
much as this 13s 4d; yet, let the lords any other time do as they think
to be most profitable in their own circumstances (77)''.

But it was not only the landlords who suffered from the depopulation of the countryside. The peasants, too, were growing
very discontented. As we shall see in the next chapter, this was soon
to come to a head.

Alexander Rey Scotore C 9 lewellin princeps wallie

A medieval Parliament: the king is seated in the centre with the bishops on
the left, the lords on the right and the commons in the middle

70

# 7 Peasant Discontent

LANDOWNERS RESENTED peasants trying to take advantage of the labour shortage. John Gower, who had been a well-to-do small landowner, complained of their attitude: "Three things, all of the same sort, are merciless when they get the upper hand: a water flood, a wasting fire, and the common multitude of small folk. For these will never be checked by reason or discipline; and therefore, to speak in brief, the present world is so troubled by them that it is well to set a remedy thereunto. Ha! age of ours, whither turnest thou? For the poor and small folk, who should cleave to their labour, demand to be better fed than their masters. Moreover, they bedeck themselves in fine colours and fine attire, whereas (were it not for their pride and privy conspiraces) they would be clad in sackcloth as of old (78)." *Landowners' complaints*

He accused them of demanding extortionate wages: "The shepherd and the cowherd demand more wages now than the master-bailiff was wont to take; and, whithersoever we look, whatsoever be the work, labourers are now of such price that, when we must needs use them, where we were wont to spend two shillings we must now spend five or six (79)." *Wage demands*

Gower looked back to the time before the Black Death when the peasants had been content with their lot: "Labourers of olden time were not wont to eat wheaten bread; their bread was of either corn or of beans, and their drink was of the spring. Then, cheese and milk were a feast to them; rarely had they other feast than this. Their garment was of hodden grey: then was the world of such folk well ordered in its estate (80)."

He called on other landowners to act before the peasants ruined

71

them all: "Now they work little, dress and feed like their betters, and ruin stares us in the face. Meseems that the lords of this land are sunk in sleep and lethargy, so that they take no heed of the madness of the common folk. Thus they suffer this nettle, that is so violent in itself, to grow. He who surveyeth this time of ours may well fear that soon—if God provide no remedy—this impatient nettle will suddenly sting us before men do justice upon it (81)."

*Law on wages*

Edward III and his council did try to check the rise in wages while the Black Death was still raging. A royal ordinance of 1349 sought to force the able-bodied to work, and to fix wage rates at their 1346 level: "Lately a great part of the people, and especially of labourers and servants, has died during the pestilence, and some, perceiving the pressing need of the lords, and the great scarcity of servants, refuse to serve unless they receive excessive wages, while others prefer to beg in idleness than to get their livelihood by labour.

"We . . . have had treaty and deliberation upon this matter with the prelates, nobles, and other experienced persons assisting us, by whose unanimous counsel we have ordained: that every man or woman in our realm of whatever condition, free or bond, being able in body, and below the age of 60 years, not living in merchandise, not exercising any craft, nor having wherewith to live of his own resources, nor land of his own in whose tillage he may employ himself, and not serving another, if he shall be required to serve in any suitable service, considering his condition, shall be bound to serve him who required him, and shall receive only such wages, allowances, hire or salary, as were accustomed to be offered in the place where he is to serve, in the twentieth year of our reign, or in the average five or six years preceding (82)."

*Statute of Labourers*

In 1351, the first Parliament held since the Black Death passed the Statute of Labourers. This made the labour laws more definite, and explained how they were to be imposed. Knighton told what was done to make the landowners observe them: "In the meantime the King sent notice into all counties of the realm that reapers and other labourers should not receive more than they had been wont, under a penalty defined by statute, and he introduced a statute for this cause. But the labourers were so arrogant and hostile that they paid no heed to the King's mandate; but if any-one wanted to have them

Richard II with his advisers during the growing peasant unrest

he was obliged to give them whatever they asked, and either to lose his fruits and crops, or satisfy their greed and arrogance.

"But the King levied heavy fines upon abbots, priors, knights of great and less degree, and others great and small throughout the countryside when it became known to him that they did not observe his ordinance, and gave higher wages to their labourers; taking 100 shillings from some, 40 shillings or 20 shillings from others, according as they were able to pay. Moreover he took 20 shillings from each plough-land throughout the kingdom, and notwithstanding this, he also took a 'fifteenth' (83)."

Steps were also taken to enforce wage restraint upon the peasants: "Then the King caused many labourers to be arrested, and sent them to prison, many of whom escaped and went away to the forests and woods for a time . . . Those who were taken were heavily fined. Others swore that they would not take wages higher than had formerly been the custom, and so were set free from prison. The same thing was done in the case of other labourers in the towns . . . (84)"

An entry in the Lincolnshire Assize Roll of 1353 shows a prosecution under the Statute of a peasant who refused to work as a serf: "The jury present that William de Caburn, of Lymbergh, ploughman, will not work except as a day labourer or a monthly labourer. And he will not eat salt meat, but only fresh meat, and for this cause he hath departed from the township, for no man dared to hire him in this fashion contrary to the statute (85)."

*Peasants*
*defiant*
Langland, writing a few years after the passing of the Statute, told how many peasants were not intimidated by such measures (86):

> *And then would Wastour not work, but wandren about . . .*
> *Labourers, that have no land to live on but their hands,*
> *Deigned not to dine to-day on yesterday's cabbage,*
> *May no penny-ale please them, nor no piece of bacon,*
> *But if it be fresh flesh or fish, fried or baked,*
> *And that hot and hotter still, to keep the chill from their maw*
> *And, but if he be highly hired, else will he chide*
> *And wail the time that ever he was workman born.*
> *And then curseth he the King, and all his Council with him,*
> *That lay down such laws, the labourers to grieve.*

*Our*
*neighbours*
*the poor*
Langland sympathised with the poorest of the peasants who faced destitution if wages stayed the same while prices rose: "The poorest folk are our neighbours, if we look about us—the prisoners in dungeons and the poor in their hovels, overburdened with children, and rack-rented by landlords. For whatever they save by spinning they spend on rent, or on milk and oatmeal to make gruel and fill the bellies of their children who clamour for food. And they themselves are often famished with hunger, and wretched with the miseries of winter—cold, sleepless nights, when they get up to rock the cradle cramped in a corner, and rise before dawn to card and comb the wool, to wash and scrub and mend, and wind yarn and peel rushes for their rushlights. The miseries of these women who dwell in hovels are too pitiful to read, or

describe in verse.

"Yet there are many more who suffer like them—men who go hungry and thirsty all day long, and strive their utmost to hide it—ashamed to beg, or tell their neighbours of their need. I've seen enough of the world to know how they suffer, these men who have many children, and no means but their trade to clothe and feed them. For many hands are waiting to grasp the few pence they earn, and while the Friars feast on roast venison, they have bread and thin ale, with perhaps a scrap of cold meat or stale fish. And on Fridays and fast days a farthing's worth of cockles or a few mussels would be a feast for such folk. I tell you, it would be a real charity to help men so burdened, and comfort these cottagers along with the blind and the lame (87)."

He attacked the greed of the landlords, who benefited from the Statute and were insensitive to the condition of the peasants (88): *Greedy landlords*

> God is deaf now-a-days and deigneth not hear us,
> And prayers have no power the Plague to stay,
> Yet the wretches of this world take no heed of it,
> Nor for dread of death withdraw them from pride,
> Nor share their plenty with the poor;
> But in gaiety, in gluttony they glut themselves with wealth,
> And the more they win, wealth and riches,
> And lord it over lands, the less they part with.

In 1377, amid the growing tension in the country, the aged Edward III died; he was succeeded by the ten-year-old Richard II. *Rebellious serfs* In his first Parliament that year several petitions were presented, alleging that serfs were witholding their services from their lords, and taking part in widespread conspiracies. This petition even envisages a peasants' revolt: "These men have refused to allow the officials of the lords to distrain them for the said customs and services; and have made confederation and alliance together to resist the lords and their officials by force, so that each will aid the other whenever they are distrained for any reason. And they threaten to kill their lords' servants if these make distraint upon them for their customs and services. The consequence is that, for fear of the deaths that might result from the rebellion and resistance of these men, the lords and their officials do not make distraint for their customs and services (89)." Rebellion was close at hand.

75

John Wycliffe (*c.* 1320–84), the Oxford scholar and church reformer

# 8 John Wycliffe and John Ball

PEASANT DISCONTENT was reaching flash point. This was hastened, unwittingly, by the teaching of John Wycliffe (*c.* 1325-84), an Oxford scholar who wished to reform the Church. From 1377 Wycliffe called on the Church to give up its property and live in evangelical poverty on the alms of the faithful. This is how the *Chronicon Angliae* summarized his teaching: "And among other unspeakable things, he denied that the Pope is able to excommunicate anyone . . . and said, moreover, that neither the King nor any secular lord could give property in perpetuity to any person or church; because if such should habitually commit sin, temporal lords might meritoriously take away from them what they had previously given—which, he said, was practised in the time of William Rufus . . . He asserted, moreover, that, if they stood in need, temporal lords might lawfully lay claim to the goods of possessioners to relieve their own want (90)."

*Wycliffe's teaching*

Wycliffe sent out "Poor Priests" nicknamed "Lollards" or "babblers" to take his teaching to the people. But many of them carried his ideas further than he intended and denounced the landowners as well as the Church. An unfriendly satirist wrote (91):

*The Lollards*

> All stipends they forbid to give
> And tithes whereon poor curates live.
> From sinful lords their dues they take;
> Bid serfs their services forsake.

Alarmed by the words of these Lollards, Wycliffe quickly denied that peasants could refuse to serve their lords: "The fiend [devil] moveth some men to say that Christian men should not be servants or thralls to heathen lords, since they would be false to God and

77

less worthy than Christian men. Neither to Christian lords—for they be brethren in kind, and Jesus Christ bought Christian men on the Cross and made them free. But against this heresy Paul writeth in God's law (92)."

Wycliffe insisted that the preaching of the Poor Priests had been misinterpreted: "But yet, some men that ben out of charity, slander Poor Priests with this error, that servants or tenants may lawfully withhold rents or services from their lords, when lords ben openly wicked in their living (93)."

*Wycliffe supports serfs*
At the same time, Wycliffe was not afraid to side with the serfs who demanded freedom and to show anger at their oppression by the landlords: "Strifes, contests and debates have been used in our land, for lords strive with their tenants to bring them in thraldom more than they should by reason and charity. Also, lords many times do wrongs to poor men by extortions and unreasonable amercements [fines] and unreasonable taxes, and take poor men's goods, and pay not therefore but with sticks [tallies], and despise them and menace and sometime beat them when they ask their pay.

"And thus lords devour poor men's goods in gluttony and waste and pride, and they perish for mischief and hunger and thirst and cold, and their children also. And if their rent be not readily paid their beasts are distressed, and they pursued without mercy, though they be never so poor and needy . . . (94)"

*John Ball*
The chief agitator on behalf of the peasants was a priest, John Ball. He had first worked at St. Mary's Abbey in York and then at Colchester. He became a popular preacher. The *Chronicon Angliae* expressed the common belief that Ball was a disciple of Wycliffe: "For twenty years and more this man had been preaching continually in different places such things as he knew were pleasing to the people, speaking ill of both ecclesiastics and secular lords, and had rather won the goodwill of the common people than merit in the sight of God.

"For he taught the people that tithes ought not to be paid unless he who should give them were richer than the rector or vicar who received them; and that tithes and offerings ought to be withheld if the parishioner were known to be a man of better life than his curate; and also that none were fit for the Kingdom of God who were not born in matrimony.

"He taught, moreover, the perverted doctrines of the perfidious John Wycliffe, and the opinions that he held, with many more that it would be tedious to recite . . . Being prohibited by the bishops from preaching in churches, he took to speaking in streets and villages and in the open fields. Nor did he lack hearers among the common people, whom he always strove to entice to his sermons by pleasing words, and slander of the prelates (95)."

Ball was condemned by his superiors in the Church, and often *Ball* thrown in prison. The Register of the Archbishop of Canterbury *denounced* contains this decree of 1366, about Ball's preaching, addressed to the Dean of Bocking in Essex: "It has come to our hearing by common report that one John Ball, pretending to be a priest, is preaching manifold errors and scandals within our said jurisdiction, as well to the ruin of his own soul and the souls of his adherents as to the manifest scandal of the whole Church. Being unwilling, therefore, to tolerate this hurt, we order you to [forbid] any to be present at the preaching of the said John, on pain of greater excommunication . . . And denouncing all who shall offend against it . . . you shall cite them to appear before us . . . You shall also cite . . . the said John to appear personally before us, to make answer concerning certain articles and interrogations to be put before him touching the correction and safety of his soul (96)."

John Ball, however, was not to be deterred. Froissart wrote: *A rousing* "A mad priest in the county of Kent, John Ball by name, had for *sermon* some time been encouraging these notions, and had several times been confined in the Archbishop of Canterbury's prison for his absurd speeches. For it was his habit on Sundays after mass, when everyone was coming out of church, to collect a crowd round him in the market place and address them more or less as follows:

" 'My friends, the state of England cannot be right until everything is held communally, and until there is no distinction between nobleman and serf, and we are all as one. Why are those whom we call lords masters over us? How have they deserved it? By what right do they keep us enslaved? We are all descended from our first parents, Adam and Eve; how then can they say that they are better lords than us, except in making us toil and earn for them to spend? They are dressed in velvet and furs, while we wear only cloth. They have wine, and spices and good bread, while we have rye, and straw that has been thrown away, and water to drink. They have fine houses and manors, and we have to brave the wind and rain as we toil in the fields. It is by the sweat of our brows that they maintain their high state. We are called serfs, and we are beaten if we do not perform our tasks. We have no sovereign to appeal to, or to listen to us and give us justice. Let us go to the King. He is young, and we will show him our miserable slavery, we will tell him it must be changed, or else we will provide the remedy ourselves. When the King sees us, either he will listen to us, or we will help ourselves' (97).''

Lollards, Wycliffe's followers, being taken to their execution

1381: summer
of conspiracy
By 1381 Ball had gathered many supporters around him. That summer he sent messengers to the towns and villages of southern England, calling on everyone to prepare for a march on London: "With these and similar words John Ball harangued the people as they came out of mass on Sundays, and a number of ill-disposed people agreed with his theme. On being informed, the Archbishop of Canterbury again had John Ball imprisoned for two or three months, but it would have been better had he locked him up for the rest of his life, or even had him executed. But the Archbishop could not in all conscience put him to death, and so he was released, and at once went back to his former errors.

"A number of the meaner sort in London came to hear of his words and deeds, and in their envy of the rich began to murmur to each other that the country was badly governed, and that all

John Ball, the rebel priest, demanded even more radical social changes
than Wycliffe

the silver and gold was in the possession of the nobles. These
people began to rebel and to send word round the neighbouring
counties encouraging those of the same opinion to come at once to
London, and they would all press the King so hard that there would
not be a slave left in England (98)."

The missives conveyed by these messengers contained codewords
which would only be understood by Ball's followers. This one was

sent out to the villages of Kent and Essex (99):

*John Ball*
*Greeteth you all,*
*And doth you to understand*
*He hath rung your bell.*
*Now with right and might,*
*Will and skill,*
*God speed every dell!*

This is another: "John Ball, St. Mary's priest, greeteth well all manner of men and biddeth them in the name of the Trinity, Father, Son and Holy Ghost, stand manlike together in truth, and help truth, and truth shall help you (100):

*Now reigneth price in price,*
*Covetise is holden wise,*
*Lechery without shame,*
*Gluttony without blame,*
*Envy reigneth with reason*
*And sloth is taken in great season.*
*God do bote [amend] for now is time."*

And this message, written under a false name and address to the men of Essex, was found in the pocket of a rioter who was condemned to be hanged. "John Schep, sometime Saint Mary's priest of York, and now of Colchester, greets well John Nameless and John the Miller and John Carter and bids them that they beware of guile in the town, and stand together in God's name . . . And take with you John Trueman and all his fellows and more, and look sharp you to your own head and no more (101):

*John the Miller hath ground small, small, small.*
*The King's Son of Heaven shall pay for all.*
*Beware or you will be in woe*
*Know your true friend from your foe.*
*Have enough and say 'Hello!'*
*And do well and better and flee from sin,*
*And seek true peace and hold therein.*
*And so bids John Trueman and all his fellows."*

The peasants, as Froissart recognized, were now on the brink of rebellion: "The wretched peasantry of these counties now began

The defeat of the *Jacquerie*, the French peasant rebels, at Meaux

to rebel, saying that the servitude in which they were kept was excessive, and that at the beginning of the world no man was a slave; nor ought anyone to be treated as such, unless he had committed some treason against his master, as Lucifer did against God. But they themselves had done no such thing, and were not angels or spirits, but men of the same stuff as their masters, who treated them like beasts. This they would no longer endure: if they were to work for their masters then they must be paid (102)."

Mindful of the revolts of the peasants or *Jacques* which had occurred in France in 1358, Froissart saw the danger. But he was surprised at the event which actually sparked off the rising: "Great commotions and disturbances arose in England among the poorer people, and the country came near to complete ruin. Indeed, never was any country in such danger; for a rebellion was fostered similar to that stirred up in France by the Jacquerie, which did such damage to the country. It is strange how insignificant was its origin, which I will describe from the best of my information, as a warning to mankind (103)." This was the poll tax.

# 9 The Flame of Rebellion

THE IMMEDIATE CAUSE of the outbreak of the Peasants' Revolt was *Poll tax* the government's decision to raise badly-needed money by poll taxes. These were levied on every person (by the poll, or head) and graduated according to rank and wealth. Parliament voted three poll taxes between 1377 and 1380. This extract is from the vote of the third tax of 1380: "First the lords and commons have agreed that, for the aforesaid necessities, there shall be given from every lay person in the realm, male or female, of whatever estate or condition, above the age of fifteen years, three groats; save very beggars, who shall not be charged . . .

"So always that the levy be made in such ordinance and form, that every lay person be charged . . . in manner as follows, to wit, that towards the sum total accounted in each township, the richer shall aid the poorer, in such wise that the richest shall not pay beyond the sum of sixty groats for himself and his wife, and none shall pay less than one groat for himself and his wife.

"And that no person be charged to pay save where he and his wife and children dwell, or where he resides in service. And that all artificers, labourers, servants, and other lay persons . . . shall be each assessed and tallaged according to the rate of his condition. And that commissions be made to certain persons, to be collectors and controllers of the aforesaid sum . . . (104)"

Coming on top of their other grievances, these new taxes aroused deep resentment among the peasants. A jingle of the time ran (105):

> *Tax has troubled us all,*
> *Probat hoc mors tot validorum.*
> *The King thereof had small,*
> *Fuit in manibus cupidorum.*

85

*Opposite* A priest collecting market tolls. New taxation was the spark that set off the Peasants' Revolt

Widespread tax evasion took place. The royal council appointed special commissioners in March, 1381, to enforce full payment of the tax. For example, the commissioners for Norfolk were told: "You are to certify to the Treasurer and Barons of the Exchequer with all possible speed the number and names of all persons whom you find in each vill and parish; and you shall bring to the Exchequer your parts of the said indentures. You are to seize and arrest all those whom you find acting in opposition or rebellion to the above commands. Such men are to be held in our prisons where they are to stay until we make provision for their punishment (106)."

The revolt began, according to the *Anonimal Chronicle*, on 30th May, 1381. On that day a commissioner, Thomas Bampton, summoned the men of the three Thames-side villages of Fobbing, Corringham and Stanford to the town of Brentwood in Essex to enquire who among them had evaded the tax in January: "He had summoned before him the townships of a neighbouring hundred, and wished to have from them new contributions, commanding the people of those townships to make diligent inquiry, and give their answers, and pay their due. Among these townships was Fobbing, whose people made answer that they would not pay a penny more, because they already had a receipt from himself for the said subsidy. On which the said Thomas threatened them angrily, and he had with him two sergeants-at-arms of our lord the King (107)."

The men of Fobbing were joined by those of neighbouring Corringham and Stanford: "Then the people of these three townships came together to the number of a hundred or more, and with one assent went to the said Thomas Bampton, and roundly gave him answer that they would have no traffic with him, nor give him a penny. On which the said Thomas commanded his sergeants-at-arms to arrest these folks, and put them in prison. But the commons made insurrection against him, and would not be arrested, and went about to kill the said Thomas and the said sergeants.

"On this Thomas fled towards London to the King's Council; but the commons took to the woods, for fear that they had of his malice, and they hid there some time, till they were almost famished, and afterwards they went from place to place to stir up other people to rise against the lords and great folk of the country (108)."

The young King Richard's advisers sent Sir Robert Belknap, *First* Chief Justice of the King's Bench, into Essex to restore order. *bloodshed* Belknap swore in jurors among the local people to make statements about the offenders. But "the commons rose against him, and came before him, and told him that he was a traitor to the King, and that it was of pure malice that he would put them in default, by means of false inquests made before him. And they took him, and made him swear on the Bible that never again would he hold such a session, nor act as a justice in such inquests. And they made him give them a list of the names of all the jurors, and they took all the jurors they could catch, and cut off their heads, and cast their houses to the ground. So the said Sir Robert took his way home without delay.

"And afterwards the said commons assembled together, before Whitsunday, to the number of some 50,000, and they went to the manors and townships of those who would not rise with them, and cast their houses to the ground or set fire to them. At this time they caught three clerks of Thomas Bampton, and cut off their heads, and carried the heads about with them for several days stuck on poles as an example to others. For it was their purpose to slay all lawyers, and all jurors, and all the servants of the King whom they could find (109)."

The flame of revolt now spread throughout Essex. The story is *Essex aflame* told in the *Chronicon Angliae*: "The peasants, whom we call villeins or bondsmen, with the rural inhabitants in Essex, coveting greater things, and in hopes of reducing everything into subjection to themselves, came together in a great multitude and began to make great tumult, demanding their liberty . . . They intended in future to be bound to pay service to no man.

"The men of two villages, who were the authors and prime movers in this mischief, sent word to each village that all, old and young, should flock to them, furnished with such arms as they could get; and that those who did not come, or despised this warning would have their goods destroyed, their houses set on fire or pulled down, and their heads cut off. These terrible threats made all hasten to them, so that in a short time so great a number was assembled that it was estimated at some 5000, of the meanest common people and peasants . . . (110)"

The parson *above*, and the shipman *opposite*, two of Chaucer's Canterbury pilgrims. Rebels in Kent made all the pilgrims swear loyalty to the King and the commons

*Rebellion in Kent*     The Essex rebels sent messengers to the people of Kent, who rose in arms a few days later: "When the men of Kent heard news of what they had long hoped for, they too without delay gathered together a large band of commons and peasants, by the same devices wherewith the Essex men had collected their bands . . . In a short time [they] stirred up the whole of their county to a similar tumult. And soon they besieged all the roads by which pilgrims go to Canterbury, and stopping all the pilgrims they compelled them to swear: first to be faithful to King Richard and the commons . . . then that they would be ready to come and join

them whenever they should please to send for them; that they would persuade all their fellow-citizens and neighbours to hold with them, and would consent to the raising of no taxes in the realm in future save the 'fifteenths' which alone their fathers and fore-fathers knew and submitted to (111)."

Throughout Kent the rebels released prisoners from the jails. These included John Ball, then in the Archbishop of Canterbury's prison at Maidstone: "At last, having been excommunicated, yet not desisting, he was thrown into prison, where he predicted that he would be set free by 20,000 of his friends—which afterwards

RICARDVS

happened in the great disturbances, when the commons broke open all the prisons, and made the prisoners depart (112)."

Joined by John Ball, the Kentish rebels decided to march on London. On 10th June they were joined by two other leaders, Wat Tyler and Jack Straw, as recounted by Froissart: "On the Monday before the feast of Corpus Christi, 1381, these men left their homes and set out for London, to speak to the King and to gain their freedom, for their object was that no Englishman should remain a serf. At Canterbury they found John Ball (he was looking, in vain, for the archbishop, who was in London with the King) and with him Wat Tyler and Jack Straw. They were given a warm welcome, for the people of Canterbury were on their side; and having decided to make for London to see the King, they sent word to their supporters in Essex and Sussex, and as far as Bedford and Stafford, encouraging them to do the same, so that London would be surrounded. In this way the King would be unable to escape them; they aimed to assemble together in London from every side on the feast of Corpus Christi (113)." *March on London*

Canterbury, too, was occupied by a group of rebels on 10th June. For the next month, it was the stronghold of the revolt: "At Canterbury, they invaded the church of Saint Thomas and did great damage; they also wrecked the apartments of the Archbishop, saying as they destroyed or removed his belongings: 'This chancellor of England has had his furniture cheap. He will now give us an account of the revenues of the country, and of the great sums he has raised since the King's coronation.' *Rebels in Canterbury*

"After raiding the monasteries of Saint Thomas and Saint Vincent, they left for Rochester, accompanied by all the inhabitants of Canterbury. They were joined by the people of the villages to right and left of the road, and they advanced like a whirlwind, mercilessly destroying the houses of attorneys and King's proctors, and of the officers of the Archbishop's court (114)."

Another group attacked Rochester Castle. They frightened the garrison into surrender, and took the governor with them: "At Rochester they were again welcomed, and they went to the castle and seized the governor, Sir John Newton, saying: 'You will have to come with us and be our commander-in-chief, and do exactly as we say.' Sir John tried to refuse, and gave a number of excellent *The fall of Rochester Castle*

91

*Opposite* King Richard II. He was only fifteen at the time of the Peasants' Revolt

reasons for doing so, but in vain, for they replied: 'Sir John, if you refuse, you are a dead man.' Realizing that the people were out of their minds and quite ready to kill him, he reluctantly put himself at their head (115)."

*Blackheath*    They marched on to Blackheath, seven miles south-east of London, killing and burning houses on the way and showing especial hatred towards lawyers for their part in enforcing the Statute of Labourers: "After leaving Rochester the rebels crossed the river and came to Dartford, never sparing the property of attorneys or proctors as they went. They cut off several heads on their way, and soon reached Blackheath, where they encamped on a hill, saying that they were for the King and the commons of England (116)."

By 12th June large numbers of Kentish men had assembled on Blackheath, while the Essex men had reached Mile End, then a hamlet outside the City walls: "And on the vigil of Corpus Christi Day the commons of Kent came to Blackheath, three leagues from London, to the number of 50,000 to wait for the King, and they displayed two banners of St. George and forty pennons. And the commons of Essex came on the other side of the water to the number of 60,000 to aid them, and to have their answer from the King (117)."

*King in*    Meanwhile, Richard II had come to London. He was lodged for
*the Tower*    safety in the Tower, where he held a meeting of the Council to consider the crisis: "At this time the King was at Windsor, but he removed with all the haste he could to London: and the Mayor and the good folks of London came to meet him, and conducted him in safety to the Tower of London. There all the Council assembled and all the lords of the land round about, that is to say, the Archbishop of Canterbury, Chancellor of England, the Bishop of London, and the Master of the Hospital of St. John's, Clerkenwell, who was then Treasurer of England, and the Earls of . . . Kent, Arundel, Warwick, Suffolk, Oxford, and Salisbury, and others to the number of six hundred (118)."

# 10 March and Massacre

THE KENTISH REBELS at once sent their hostage, the Governor of Rochester Castle, to the King with a message: "Sir John Newton was dispatched from Blackheath to speak to the King at the Tower, asking him to come and address the rebels, and informing him that all their actions were performed in his service. For the country had of recent years been sadly misgoverned, to the dishonour of the realm and the detriment of the common people by his uncles, by the clergy, and most of all by the Archbishop of Canterbury, the chancellor, from whom they wanted an account of his ministry (119)." *Message to King Richard*

Newton conveyed their wish for a meeting with the King: "Sir John did not dare refuse, but crossed the river to the Tower. The King, and those with him, were in a state of great suspense, and everyone made way for him as he landed . . . And kneeling before the King, he said: 'Most honoured sire, do not be displeased with me for the message I bring, for my dear lord, it is not of my own free will that I bring it.' 'No, Sir John,' replied the King. 'Tell us your message; we hold you excused.' *Meeting demanded*

"'Most honoured Sire, the commoners of your realm have sent me to entreat you to come and speak to them at Blackheath. They want to hear no one but yourself. You need have no fears for your person; they will do you no harm, since they are and will always continue to be your loyal subjects. They will only tell you a number of things which they say you ought to hear, but of which they have not charged me to inform you. My dear lord, have the goodness to give me an answer that will satisfy them and will convince them that I have come before you; for they hold my children as hostages,

93

and will kill them if I do not return' (120).''

Newton was told that Richard would see the rebels the next day: "The King replied: 'You shall have an answer at once.' He then held a council, at which he was advised to say that if they would come down to the river Thames on Thursday morning he would speak to them without fail. Sir John Newton conveyed this message to them, and it gave great pleasure. The rebels, who now numbered 60,000, encamped and spent the night as best they could (121)."

Next day, before their meeting with the King, the rebels were stirred by a sermon from John Ball. Ball had been prominent among them ever since his release from prison: "And when he had thus been set free, he followed them, egging them on to commit greater mischiefs, and saying that such things must surely be done. And, to corrupt the more with his doctrine, at Blackheath, where 20,000 of the commons were gathered together, he began a discourse in this fashion:

> *When Adam delved and Eve span,*
> *Who was then the gentleman?*

"And continuing his sermon, he strove to prove by the words of the proverb that he had taken for his text, that from the beginning all men were created equal by nature, and that servitude had been introduced by the unjust oppression of evil men, against the will of God, who, if it had pleased Him to create serfs, surely in the beginning of the world would have appointed who should be a serf and who a lord.

"Let them consider, therefore, that He had now given them the hour wherein, laying aside the yoke of long servitude, they might, if they wished enjoy their liberty... They must be prudent, hastening to act after the manner of a good husbandman, tilling his field, and uprooting the tares that are wont to destroy the grain; first killing the great lords of the realm, then slaying the lawyers, justices and jurors, and finally rooting out everyone whom they knew to be harmful to the community in future (122)."

The *Chronicon Angliae* went on: "And when he had preached these and many other ravings, he was in such high favour with the people that they cried out that he should be Archbishop and Chancellor, and that he alone was worthy of the office, for the

*Opposite* The Tower of London, where King Richard and his advisers sought refuge from the rebels

Les nouuelles d'Albion
S'il vous en plaist escoute
Mon frere z mon compaing
Sachez qua mon retour
...

present Archbishop was a traitor to the realm and the commons, and should be beheaded wherever he could be found (123)."

King Richard was rowed down the Thames to meet the rebels at Rotherhithe: "On the feast of Corpus Christi, the King heard mass in the chapel of the Tower, with all his lords, and afterwards embarked in his barge, with the Earls of Salisbury, Warwick, and Oxford, and other knights. They were rowed downstream to Rotherhithe, where over 10,000 men had assembled from Blackheath. When they saw the royal barge approaching, they set up such a hue and cry that it sounded as if all the devils in hell had been let loose. They had brought Sir John Newton with them, and they would have hacked him to pieces, as they had threatened, if the King had failed to appear (124)."

After a brief exchange with the noisy crowd, however, the royal party returned to the safety of the Tower: "When the King and his lords saw the hostile state of the crowd, there was none of them so bold as not to feel alarm. The King was advised not to land, but to have his barge rowed up and down the river in front of the crowd. 'Tell me what you want,' cried the King. 'I have come here to talk with you.' That part of the crowd that was nearest him answered with one voice: 'We want you to land, and then we can tell you more easily what we require.' The Earl of Salisbury then answered for the King: 'Gentlemen, you are in no fit state nor are you properly dressed to speak to the King.' Nothing more was said, and the King was conducted back to the Tower (125)."

The rebels, angry and hungry, now made for London: "When the people saw that they could achieve nothing more, they returned, in a rage, to Blackheath, where the bulk of the mob still was, and explained what had happened. Then they all cried out: 'Let us go to London!' They set out at once, and destroyed on the way a number of houses belonging to lawyers, courtiers, and the clergy; and on reaching the suburbs of London, which are extensive and beautiful, they destroyed several fine houses. In particular they demolished the Marshalsea (the King's prison) and liberated all who were confined in it. Altogether, they did great damage in the suburbs and threatened those who had closed the gates of London Bridge, saying that they would burn all the suburbs, take London by force, and burn and destroy everything (126)."

*Opposite* King Richard confronting the rebels at Rotherhithe

Richard ij allant à la rencontre des serfs anglais révoltés

The *Anonimal Chronicle* described how sympathizers in South-wark helped the Kentish rebels over London Bridge into the City. The rebels "went on to the bridge to pass into the City, but the Mayor was ready before them, and had the chains drawn up, and the drawbridge lifted, to prevent their passage. And the commons of Southwark rose with them and cried to the custodians of the bridge to lower the drawbridge and let them in, or otherwise they should be undone. And for fear that they had of their lives, the custodians let them enter, much against their will (127)."

Other groups of rebels were not prevented from entering the City gates. According to Froissart, the authorities were too scared to resist them: "The peasants in Essex, Kent, Sussex and Bedford therefore flocked to London, to the number of 60,000 in all. The chief rabble-rouser was Wat Tyler, and under him were two other leaders, Jack Straw and John Ball. This Wat had been a tiler of roofs; he was a bad character, and a deeply embittered man.

"All London, except for the rebels, was in terror. When they approached the city, the mayor and the richer citizens held council and decided to close the gates of the city and let no one enter; but they decided on reflection that there would then be a danger of all the suburbs being burned to the ground. So the city remained open to them, and they entered in troops of anything from twenty to two hundred depending on the size of the towns from which they came (128)."

*Orgy of destruction*    The City Letter Book of London told of the mob in the streets. The mob destroyed several buildings, including the Palace of the Savoy in the Strand, which belonged to John of Gaunt, Duke of Lancaster, the King's uncle and the most powerful man in the kingdom. They also destroyed the Priory of St. John at Clerkenwell because Sir Robert Hales, the Treasurer of England, was also Master of the Order: "By the aid also of perfidious commoners within the City, of their own condition, who rose in countless numbers there, they suddenly entered the City together, and, passing straight through it, went to the mansion of Sir John, Duke of Lancaster, called 'Le Savoye', and completely levelled the same with the ground, and burned it. From thence they turned to the Church of the Hospital of St. John of Jerusalem, without Smithfield, and burned and levelled nearly all the houses there, the church

98

excepted (129)."

They also ransacked the Temple, the headquarters of the lawyers *Sacking the Temple* of England. They burned the many books and records and charters they found there, since these contained records of the feudal services due to lords of the manor by serfs: "Afterwards they went to the Temple to destroy the tenants of the said Temple; and they threw the houses to the ground and cast down the tiles so that the houses were left roofless and in a poor state. They also went into the church, seized all the books, rolls and remembrances kept in the cupboards of the apprentices of the law within the Temple, carried them into the high road, and burned them there (130)."

In the evening the rebels encamped in the open space around *The Tower* the Tower. They "announced that they would not leave until they had obtained from the King all that they wanted; and that the chancellor of England must give them an account of all the revenue levied in England for the last five years; and that if he could not give a satisfactory account it would be the worse for him (131)."

Inside the Tower, as flames from the burning buildings lit up the night sky, the young King Richard anxiously sought the advice of his nobles: "At this time the King was in a turret of the great Tower of London, and could see the manor of the Savoy and the Hospital of Clerkenwell, and the house of Simon Hosteler near Newgate, and John Butterwick's place, all on fire at once. And he called all his lords about him to his chamber, and asked counsel what they should do in such necessity. And none of them could or would give him any counsel, wherefore the young King said that he would send to the Mayor of the City, to bid him order the sheriffs and aldermen to have it cried round their wards that every man between the age of fifteen and sixty, on pain of life and members, should go next morning (which was Friday) to Mile End, and meet him there at seven o'clock (132)."

The next morning, the King set out for Mile End, but a mob *Storming the Tower* broke into the Tower: "Most of the common people from the villages set out, but not all; for a great part of the mob only wanted to riot, to destroy the nobility, and to plunder the city. They clearly showed that this was the chief purpose of their rebellion; for when the gates of the Tower were opened and the King came out with his two brothers and a number of attendant lords, four hundred of the

The Archbishop of Canterbury is murdered by the rebels

mob, led by Tyler, Straw, and Ball, dashed in by force and rushed from room to room (133)."

There they murdered Simon Sudbury, Archbishop of Canterbury, who was also Lord Chancellor and much concerned with the introduction of the poll tax: "During this time the Archbishop sang his mass devoutly in the Tower, and shrived [assigned penance to] the Prior of the Hospitallers and others, and then he heard two masses or three and chanted the *Commendacione*, and the *Placebo*, and the *Dirige*, and the Seven Psalms, and a Litany, and when he was at the words 'Omnes sancti orate pro nobis', the commons burst in, and dragged him out of the chapel of the Tower, and struck and hustled him rudely, as they did also the others who were with him, and dragged them to Tower Hill (134)."

*Archbishop slain*

Flemish weavers, who were also victims of the Kentish rebels' wrath

Together with the Archbishop, they beheaded Sir Robert Hales and other royal advisers: "All of whom they beheaded in the place called 'Tourhille' [Tower Hill], without the said Tower; and then carrying their heads through the City upon lances, they set them up on London Bridge, fixing them there on stakes (135)."

*Flemings massacred*

The rebels also killed many prominent citizens and Flemish weavers, who had been invited into England by Edward II to establish better methods of cloth manufacture. These men were unpopular because they were thought to be sending gold out of the country: "Upon the same day there was also no little slaughter within the City, as well of natives as of aliens. Richard Lions, citizen and vintner of the said City, and many others, were beheaded in Chepe. In the Vintry also, there was a very great massacre of Flemings, and in one heap there were lying about forty headless bodies of persons who had been dragged forth from the churches and their houses; and hardly was there a street in the City in which there were not bodies lying of those who had been slain. Some of the houses also in the said city were pulled down, and others in the suburbs destroyed, and some too, burned (136)."

*Chaucer remembers*

Geoffrey Chaucer recalled this massacre in the *Nun's Priest's Tale* when he described the farm servants chasing a fox (137):

*So hideous was the noise—God bless us all,*
*Jack Straw and all his followers in their brawl*
*Were never half so shrill, for all their noise,*
*When they were murdering those Flemish boys.*

# 11 King Richard and Wat Tyler

"THE KING made his way to Mile End, but was not accompanied by his brothers, the Earl of Kent and Sir John Holland, who did not dare show themselves to the people there, as they feared for their lives. When the King arrived, he found 60,000 men assembled from different villages and districts of England. He advanced towards them, and asked them pleasantly: 'My friends, I am your King and your lord. What do you want? And what do you wish to say?' Those who heard him replied: 'We want you to set us free for ever, us and our descendants and our lands, and to grant that we should never again be called serfs, nor held in bondage' (138)."

*Meeting at Mile End*

There Richard made them promises which included the abolition of serfdom throughout the country: "And at this time the King made the commons draw themselves out in two lines . . . He proclaimed to them that he would confirm and grant it that they should be free, and generally should have their will, and that they might go through all the realm of England and catch all traitors and bring them to him in safety, and then he would deal with them as the law demanded (139)."

*Royal promises*

Letters containing the King's promises were drawn up. The representatives of each county present were given a royal banner as a proof of his protection: "All the innocent and well-intentioned people were quite satisfied by these words, and began to return to London. The King promised a banner to each of the following counties—Kent, Essex, Sussex, Bedford, Cambridge, Stafford and Lincoln. He gave a free pardon for all that had been done by the people of these counties, on condition that they followed the royal banner back to their homes on the terms he had mentioned. Half

103

A Benedictine abbot of the time

All clergy, including the friars, were unpopular with the rebel peasants

of the mob dispersed, and the King gave orders for thirty secretaries to draw up the letters that very day, and for the letters to be sealed and delivered (140)."

To the dismay of the authorities, a large group of the rebels refused to budge from London: "The chief mischief-makers, however, remained: Tyler, Straw, and Ball declared that though the people were satisfied, they themselves would not depart. And with them there remained over 30,000 who took the same view; they stayed in the city, showing no inclination to receive the King's letters, but keeping London in a state of terror. The citizens kept to their houses, with as many of their friends and attendants as they could muster (141)." *Refusal to disperse*

The next morning, the massacre continued. Among those killed was the Marshal of the Marshalsea Prison in Southwark; he was taken in Westminster Abbey at nine o'clock when the monks were saying Terce, the third service of the day: "The next morning, Saturday, great numbers of the commons came into Westminster *Terror continues*

105

Abbey at the hour of Terce, and there they found John Imworth, Marshal of the Marshalsea and warden of the prisoners, a tormentor without pity; he was at the shrine of St. Edward, embracing a marble pillar, to crave aid and succour from the saint to preserve him from his enemies. But the commons wrenched his arms away from the pillar of the shrine, and dragged him away to Cheapside, and there beheaded him (142)."

*King at Westminster Abbey*

That afternoon the King went in procession to Westminster Abbey: "And on this same day, at three in the afternoon, the King came to the Abbey of Westminster, and some 200 persons with him . . . The abbot and monks of the said Abbey, and the canons and vicars of St. Stephen's Chapel, came to meet him in procession clothed in their copes and their feet naked, half way to Charing Cross. And they brought him to the Abbey, and then to the High Altar of the church, and the King made his prayer devoutly and left an offering for the altar and the relics. And afterwards he spoke with the anchorite, and confessed to him, and remained with him some time. Then the King caused a proclamation to be made that all the commons of the country who were still in London should come to Smithfield, to meet him there; and so they did (143)."

*At Smithfield*

The meeting was arranged to take place at Smithfield, an open space just outside the City. Smithfield seemed safer than Mile End because it was surrounded on all sides by buildings including St. Bartholomew's Church and Hospital: "The King rode past Saint Bartholomew's Church in Smithfield, and found the remainder of the rabble assembled in the horse market. The King's banners had been given them on the previous evening, but they intended to pillage the city that very day (144)."

*Wat Tyler*

The rebels were led on this occasion by Wat Tyler. The King asked the Mayor of London to summon Tyler to him: "And when the King and his train had arrived there they turned into the Eastern meadow in front of St. Bartholomew's which is a house of canons: and the commons arrayed themselves on the west side in great battles. At this moment the Mayor of London, William Walworth, came up, and the King bade him go to the commons, and make their chieftain come to him (145)."

The familiarity with which Tyler treated the King shocked the writer of the *Anonimal Chronicle*: "He came to the King with great

King Richard II takes command of the rebels at Smithfield in London

confidence, mounted on a little horse, that the commons might see
him. And he dismounted, holding in his hand a dagger which he
had taken from another man, and when he had dismounted he
half bent his knee, and then took the King by the hand, and shook

*Overleaf* Wat Tyler is struck down by one of King Richard's knights after
insulting the King

his arm forcibly and roughly, saying to him, 'Brother, be of good comfort and joyful, for you shall have, in the fortnight that is to come, praise from the commons even more than you have yet had, and we shall be good companions' (146)."

The King tried to calm him, but Tyler seemed only able to repeat demands to which the King had already agreed at Mile End: "And the King said to Walter, 'Why will you not go back to your own country?' But the other answered, with a great oath, that neither he nor his fellows would depart until they had got their charter such as they wished to have it, and had certain points rehearsed, and added to their charter which they wished to demand. And he said in a threatening fashion that the lords of the realm would rue it bitterly if these points were not settled to their pleasure (147)."

The King tried to end the meeting in a friendly manner: "The King gave an easy answer, and said that he should have all that he could fairly grant, reserving only for himself the regality of his crown. And then he bade him go back to his home, without making further delay (148)."

*Tyler provoked*  Tyler continued to act rudely. The King's attendants now answered him back as if they were picking a quarrel. Tyler "sent for a flagon of water to rinse his mouth because of the great heat he was in and, when it was brought, he rinsed his mouth in a very rude and disgusting fashion before the King's face. And then he made them bring him a jug of ale and drank a great draught; and then, in the presence of the King, he climbed on his horse again. At this time a certain squire from Kent, who was among the King's retinue . . . saw him [Tyler] and said aloud that he knew him for the greatest thief and robber in Kent (149)."

*Tyler wounded*  That did it. "For these words Tyler tried to strike him with his dagger, and would have slain him in the King's presence. But because he strove to do so, the Mayor of London, William Walworth, reasoned with Tyler for his violent behaviour in the King's presence, and arrested him. And because he arrested him, Tyler stabbed the Mayor with his dagger in the stomach in great wrath. But, as it pleased God, the Mayor was wearing armour (under his robes) and took no harm, but like a hardy and vigorous man drew his sword and struck back at Tyler, and gave him a deep cut on the neck, and then a great cut on the head. And during this scuffle one of the King's followers drew his sword and ran Tyler two or three times through the body, mortally wounding him. And he [Tyler] spurred his horse, crying to the commons to avenge him, and the horse carried him some four score paces, and then he fell to the ground half dead (150)."

The King, as Froissart realized, was in great danger. Many of the rebels were archers, and they aimed at him their formidable longbows which had proved so deadly on the battlefields of France. Tyler's "followers then began to cry out 'They have cut down our captain! Come on, let us kill them all!' They drew themselves up in some kind of order and advanced, each with his bow ready to shoot. At great personal risk the King then rode out in front of his followers, forbidding any to follow him, and advanced on the mob, who were preparing to avenge their leader: 'Gentlemen', he said, 'what do you want? You have no other captain but me. I am your King. Keep the peace.' When they saw and heard the King speak, most of the crowd were quite abashed and the more peaceful of them began to disperse (151)." *King's coolness*

King Richard led the mob out to Clerkenwell Fields; there they were surrounded by a force of citizens hurriedly summoned by the Mayor. "Presently the aldermen came to him [the King] in a body, bringing with them their wardens, and the wards arrayed in bands, a fine company of well-armed folks in great strength. And they enveloped the commons like sheep within a pen, and after that the Mayor had set the wardens of the city on their way to the King, he returned with a company of lances to Smithfield, to make an end of the captain of the commons (152)." *Clerkenwell Fields*

The Mayor meanwhile went to look for Tyler in Smithfield. He was surprised to find him gone. "It was told him that he had been carried by some of the commons to the hospital for poor folks by St. Bartholomew's, and was put to bed in the chamber of the master of the hospital. And the Mayor went thither and found him, and had him carried out to the middle of Smithfield, in presence of his fellows, and there beheaded. And thus ended his wretched life. But the Mayor had his head set on a pole and borne before him to the King, who still abode in the Fields (153)." *Wat Tyler slain*

At Tyler's death, the revolt suddenly collapsed in London: "When the commons saw that their chieftain, Wat Tyler, was dead in such a manner, they fell to the ground there among the wheat, like beaten men, imploring the King for mercy for their misdeeds. And the King benevolently granted them mercy, and most of them took flight (154)." The citizens of London were greatly relieved.

# 12 The End of the Revolt

WHILE TYLER had been meeting the King, serious rioting had broken out in other parts of the country. In Suffolk, Sir John Cavendish, the judge and commissioner to enforce the Statute of Labourers, was murdered: "They went to Bury, and found in that town a justice, Sir John Cavendish, Chief Justice of the King's Bench, and brought him to the pillory, and cut off his head and set it on the pillory. And afterwards they dragged to the pillory the Prior of that abbey, a good man and wise, and an accomplished singer, and a certain monk with him, and cut off their heads. And they set them on poles before the pillory, that all who passed down that street might see them (155)." *East Anglian revolt*

Local forces, however, soon rallied against the rebels. In Norfolk, Henry Despenser, Bishop of Norwich, subdued them and executed their leaders without trial: "Wherefore the said Bishop, gathering in to himself many men-at-arms and archers, assailed them at several places, wherever he could find them, and captured many of them. And the Bishop first confessed them and then beheaded them (156)." *The fighting bishop*

And when rebels attacked Huntingdon, the townsmen held the bridge and inflicted heavy losses on them: "The rest was glad to fly, and went to Ramsey to pass thereby, and took shelter in the town, and sent to the abbot for victuals to refresh them. And the abbot sent them out bread, wine, beer, and other victuals, in great abundance, for he dare not do otherwise. So they ate and drank to satiety, and afterwards slept deep into the morning, to their confusion. For meanwhile the men of Huntingdon rose, and gathered to them other folks of the countryside, and suddenly fell *Routed at Ramsey* upon the commons at Ramsey and killed some twenty-four of them. The others took to headlong flight, and many of them were slain as they went through the countryside, and their heads set on high trees as an example to others (157)."

*Rebels punished*  This rough-and-ready justice was followed by the official action: "Afterwards the King sent out his messengers into divers parts, to capture the malefactors and put them to death. And many were taken and hanged at London, and they set up many gallows around the City of London, and in other cities and boroughs of the south country (158)."

*A sharp axe*  This rhyme, found in a contemporary manuscript, refers to the repression of the revolt. The "stool" is the executioner's block (159):

> *Man beware and be no fool:*
> *Think upon the axe and of the tool!*
> *The stool was hard, the axe was sharp,*
> *The fourth year of King Richard.*

*Rebels accused*  The records of courts in Kent contain examples of the charges brought against the rebels: "The jurors say on their oath that Roger Boldwyn of Boughton-under-Blean raised insurrection with other malefactors on the Wednesday next after the feast of the Holy Trinity in the fourth year of the reign of the King that now is, and was aiding and abetting when Simon, Archbishop of Canterbury was feloniously killed, and was there and then present . . .

"Also they say that John Hales . . . and other unknown malefactors made insurrection on Monday next after the feast of Holy Trinity by force and arms, and feloniously broke into the castle of our lord the King in Canterbury, and carried away divers felons that were in the said castle and prison, and took William Septvanz, the sheriff of Kent and dragged him away with them, and compelled him to deliver to them the books and writs of our lord the King. And immediately that they were delivered they burned them, to the prejudice of our lord the King and his crown. Also they say that James Grene and Richard Dale feloniously broke into the gaol of Maidstone, and took away the prisoners that were in the said gaol, to the prejudice of our lord the King and his crown (160)."

*John Ball's death*  Most of the ring-leaders were executed. John Ball did not deny the evidence against him (see p. 82): "The said John Ball confessed that he had written this letter and sent it to the commons, and admitted that he had written many more. Wherefore he was hanged at St. Albans on the 15th of July, in the King's presence (161)."

William Grindcobbe, the leader of the rising at St. Albans, was released on bail in order to pacify his followers. But he did not pacify them. Instead he declared: "Friends, who after so long an age of oppression, have at last won yourselves a short breath of freedom, hold firm while you can, and have no thought for me or what I may suffer. For if I die for the cause of the liberty that we have won, I shall think myself happy to end my life as a martyr. Act now as you would have acted supposing that I had been beheaded at Hertford yesterday (162)." Nor surprisingly, Grindcobbe was taken back to prison and executed.

*William Grindcobbe*

But on the whole, the government acted with moderation. The first executions were followed by later pardons. The pleading of Richard's new Queen, Anne of Bohemia, was probably less powerful than Knighton supposed: "In the following year, 1382, at the special request of Queen Anne and other magnates of the realm, especially the pious Duke of Lancaster, the lord King gave a general pardon to all the aforesaid rebels and malefactors, their adherents, abettors and followers. He granted charters to this effect and through God's mercy the previous madness came to an end (163)."

*General pardon*

The government at once revoked the royal charters which had been granted to the rebels. Writs to this effect were sent out to the sheriffs of the counties in July, 1381: "Although lately in the abominable disturbance . . . certain our letters patent were made at the importunate demand of these same insurgents, to the effect that we enfranchised all our liege subjects . . . granting each and all of them our firm peace; that we willed that they should be free to buy and sell in all cities, boroughs, market towns and other places within the realm; and that no acre of land in the aforesaid counties held in service or bondage should be held at more than four pence the acre . . .

*Charters revoked*

"Because, however, the said letters were issued unduly, and without mature consideration, we have recalled and annulled the said letters (164)."

The government was determined to see that all damage done during the rising should be made good. Here is an entry in the *York*

*The walls of York*

Rebuilding damaged city walls

*Memorandum Book*: "On Monday 17th June in the same year [1381] the earthen walls against the city walls were destroyed and lowered to the ground, and the great gates—both towards the Ouse and towards Kynges Toftes—were carried off by the rebellious commons of the city. And during the following Lent, Simon de Quixlay, then mayor of the city, was compelled by the King's council in chancery to renovate and repair these walls and gates at the expense of the city. Simon entered into an obligation to complete these repairs before the following 24th June under penalty of 5,000 marks (165)."

Discontent
But it was impossible to set the clock back. The conflict between landlord and tenant continued. Sporadic risings took place, such as this one in Kent in 1390: "Item, on 13th January sixteen men,

skilled in various mechanical arts, were captured at Croydon and imprisoned in the Marshalsea [Prison]. Some of them were workmen who wished to rise against churchmen as well as other lay neighbours of theirs in order to kill them. They planned to promote another rising, worse than the others already mentioned; but their schemes were too quickly revealed. And so three of these men were drawn and hanged at the gallows in February (166)."

The revolt of the English peasants had failed. But serfdom was already on the decline. Landlords found it more and more profitable to free their serfs, and hire labourers to work for them. By 1529, when Anthony Fitzherbert wrote this passage in his *Boke of Surveyenge*, serfdom had practically gone from England: "How be it, in some places the bondmen continue as yet, which seems to me the greatest inconvenience that is now suffered by the law, that is, to have any Christian man bound to another, and to have the rule of his body, land, and goods . . . For it seems to me that no man should be bound except to God, and to his king and prince over him . . . And it would be a charitable deed to manumit [set free] all that be bound, and make them free of body and blood (167)."

*Decline of serfdom*

117

# Further Reading

CONTEMPORARY ACCOUNTS of both the Black Death and the Peasants' Revolt in England are to be found in the writings of chroniclers. Some of these men were monks entrusted with the task in the larger monasteries, and in the official records of Parliament, the corporations of the larger towns, the law courts and the bishops' registries.

Of the chroniclers, four are especially important—the *Anonimal Chronicle*, written by a monk of St. Mary's Abbey, York, who seems to have witnessed the events of the revolt in London; the *Chronicon Angliae* by Thomas of Walsingham, a monk of St. Albans Abbey, the most interesting historian of his time; *Knighton's Chronicle* by Henry Knighton, a canon of St. Mary's Abbey, Leicester, who wrote the most informative description of the Black Death, though his record of the revolt is probably based largely on hearsay; and the *Chronicle of Sir John Froissart*, by a French knight, who wrote vividly of events in England, but did not witness them himself.

Such accounts can be read in various editions and translations; extracts are contained in collections of documents. Among these are G. G. Coulton, *Life in the Middle Ages* (4 vols., 1928); Dorothy Hughes, *Illustrations of Chaucer's England* (1919); and R. B. Dobson, *The Peasants' Revolt of 1381* (1970).

General histories dealing with this period in English history include G. G. Coulton, *Medieval Panorama* (1938); G. G. Coulton, *Chaucer and His England* (1908); May McKisack, *The Fourteenth Century* (1959); and Arthur Bryant, *The Age of Chivalry* (1963).

For the Black Death, both in England and abroad, Philip Ziegler, *The Black Death* (1969), contains an excellent account and many extracts from contemporary writers; it replaces all other books on the subject. On the Peasants' Revolt there is Sir Charles Oman, *The Great Revolt of 1381* (1906), which contains a translation of the *Anonimal Chronicle*; Sir G. M. Trevelyan, *England in the Age of Wycliffe* (3rd ed. 1909); Maurice Collis, *The Hurling Time* (1958), R. H. Hilton & H. Fagan, *The English Rising of 1381* (1956); and G. R. Kesteven, *The Peasants' Revolt* (1965). A full account of the revolt also appears in A. Steel, *Richard II* (1941).

# *Picture Credits*

THE PUBLISHERS wish to thank the following for their kind permission to reproduce copyright illustrations on the pages mentioned: the Mansell Collection, *frontispiece*, 15, 16, 20-21, 27, 28, 35, 37, 38, 47, 67, 76, 80, 83, 97, 100, 107; Trustees of the British Museum, *jacket*, 10, 12, 13, 14, 30, 31, 34, 40, 42, 44, 50, 52, 57, 60, 73, 95, 108-109, 116; the Radio Times Hulton Picture Library, 51, 101; Trustees of the National Portrait Gallery, 90. Other illustrations appearing in this book are the property of the Wayland Picture Library.

# Sources

(1) J. Dahmus, *The Middle Ages* (1969), p. 244.
(2) *Froissurt's Chronicles*, ed. and trans. John Joliffe (1967), pp. 236-7.
(3) R. W. Southern, *The Making of the Middle Ages* (1959), p. 109.
(4) *Ibid*, p. 109.
(5) G. G. Coulton, *Chaucer and His England* (1908), p. 262.
(6) G. G. Coulton, *The Medieval Scene* (2nd ed. 1959), p. 69.
(7) Coulton, *Chaucer and His England*, p. 283.
(8) R. B. Dobson, *The Peasants' Revolt of 1381* (1970), pp. 53-4.
(9) Geoffrey Chaucer, *The Canterbury Tales*, trans. Nevill Coghill (1951), p. 97.
(10) G. G. Coulton, *Life in the Middle Ages* (4 vols. 1928), II, p. 78.
(11) *Ibid*, I, p. 41.
(12) G. G. Coulton, *Medieval Panorama* (1938), p. 493.
(13) Philip Ziegler, *The Black Death* (Penguin ed., 1970), p. 14.
(14) *Ibid*, pp. 14-15.
(15) *Ibid*, p. 15.
(16) Dorothy Hughes, *Illustrations of Chaucer's England* (1919), p. 145.
(17) Ziegler, *op. cit.*, p. 17.
(18) Giovanni Boccaccio, *Decameron*, trans. J. M. Rigg (1930), p. 5.
(19) Ziegler, *op. cit.*, p. 19.
(20) *Decameron*, p. 8.
(21) Ziegler, *op. cit.*, p. 23.
(22) Coulton, *Medieval Panorama*, p. 494.
(23) *Decameron*, p. 8.
(24) *Ibid*, pp. 8-9.
(25) *Ibid*, p. 10.
(26) *Ibid*, pp. 10-11.
(27) *Ibid*, pp. 11-12.
(28) *Ibid*, p. 12.
(29) *Ibid*, pp. 12-13.
(30) *Ibid*, p. 14.
(31) Ziegler, *op. cit.*, p. 58.
(32) *Ibid*, pp. 79-80.
(33) *Ibid*,, p. 81.
(34) *Ibid*, p. 67.
(35) Hughes, *Chaucer's England*, p 150.
(36) Ziegler, *op. cit.*, p. 122.
(37) F. A. Gasquet, *The Black Death* (1908), p. 81.
(38) Hughes, *op. cit.*, p. 145.
(39) *Ibid*, p. 149.
(40) Ziegler, *op. cit.*, p. 141.
(41) *Ibid*, p. 128.
(42) *Ibid*, pp. 128-9.
(43) *Ibid*, p. 194.
(44) H. T. Riley, *Memorials of London and London Life in the Thirteenth, Fourteenth and Fifteenth Centuries* (1868), p. 67.
(45) Hughes, *op. cit.*, pp. 150-1.
(46) *Ibid*, pp. 149-50.
(47) *Ibid*, pp. 192-3.
(48) Ziegler, *op. cit.*, p. 167.
(49) *Ibid*, p. 168.
(50) *Ibid*, p. 168.
(51) Hughes, *op. cit.*, p. 151.
(52) L. F. R. Williams, *History of the Abbey of St. Albans* (1917), p. 166.
(53) Hughes, *op. cit.*, p. 151.
(54) Ziegler, *op. cit.*, p. 185.
(55) Dobson, *Peasant's Revolt*, p. 59.
(56) Hughes, *op. cit.*, p. 146.
(57) Ziegler, *op. cit.*, p. 186.
(58) Hughes, *op. cit.*, p. 147.
(59) Ziegler, *op. cit.*, p. 206.
(60) *Ibid*, p. 279.
(61) *Ibid*, p. 279.
(62) *Ibid*, p. 200.
(63) Arthur Bryant, *The Age of Chivalry* (1963), p. 390.
(64) Dobson, *op. cit.*, pp. 61-2.
(65) Coulton, *Medieval Pan-*

*orama*, p. 498.

(66) Hughes, *op. cit.*, pp. 159-60.

(67) *Ibid*, p. 168.

(68) *Ibid*, p. 168.

(69) *Ibid*, pp. 166-7.

(70) Ziegler, *op. cit.*, p. 263.

(71) *Ibid*, pp. 195-6.

(72) Dobson, *op. cit.*, pp. 60-1.

(73) *Ibid*, p. 61.

(74) *Ibid*, pp. 62-3.

(75) Gasquet, *Black Death*, p. 170.

(76) G. G. Coulton, *The Medieval Village* (1925), p. 87.

(77) *Ibid*, p. 446.

(78) E. B. Osborne, *The Middle Ages* (n.d.), p. 188.

(79) Coulton, *op. cit.*, p. 236.

(80) *Ibid*, p. 237.

(81) *Ibid*, p. 237.

(82) Hughes, *op. cit.*, p. 152.

(83) *Ibid*, p. 148.

(84) *Ibid*, p. 148.

(85) Coulton, *Medieval Panorama*, p. 504.

(86) *Ibid*, p. 504.

(87) William Langland, *Piers the Plowman*, trans. J. F. Goodridge (1959), p. 298.

(88) William Langland, *The Vision of Piers Plowman*, trans. A. Burrell (1912), p. 137.

(89) Dobson, *Peasants' Revolt*, p. 76.

(90) Hughes, *op. cit.*, p. 194.

(91) G. M. Trevelyan, *England in the Age of Wycliffe* (3rd ed. 1909), p. 200.

(92) *Ibid*, p. 201.

(93) *Ibid*, p. 201.

(94) *Ibid*, p. 201.

(95) Dobson, *op. cit.*, pp. 374-5.

(96) Hughes, *op. cit.*, p. 194.

(97) *Froissart*, pp. 237-8.

(98) *Ibid*, p. 238.

(99) Bryant, *Age of Chivalry*, p. 523.

(100) *Ibid*, p. 518.

(101) *Ibid*, pp. 523-4.

(102) *Froissart*, p. 237.

(103) *Ibid*, p. 236.

(104) Hughes, *op. cit.*, pp. 228-9.

(105) Trevelyan, *op. cit.*, p. 206.

(106) Dobson, *op. cit.*, pp. 121-2.

(107) Charles Oman, *The Great Revolt of 1381* (1906), p. 187.

(108) *Ibid*, p. 187.

(109) *Ibid*, p. 188.

(110) Hughes, *op. cit.*, p. 230.

(111) *Ibid*, pp. 230-1.

(112) *Ibid*, p. 232.

(113) *Froissart*, pp. 239-40.

(114) *Ibid*, p. 240.

(115) *Ibid*, p. 240.

(116) *Ibid*, p. 241.

(117) Oman, *op. cit.*, p. 191.

(118) *Ibid*, p. 191.

(119) *Froissart*, p. 241.

(120) *Ibid*, pp. 241-2.

(121) *Ibid*, p. 242.

(122) Hughes, *op. cit.*, pp. 232-3.

(123) *Ibid*, p. 233.

(124) *Froissart*, p. 243.

(125) *Ibid*, p. 243.

(126) *Ibid*, pp. 243-4.

(127) Oman, *op. cit.*, p. 194.

(128) *Froissart*, p. 238.

(129) Riley, *London Life*, p. 449.

(130) Dobson, *op. cit.*, pp. 156-7.

(131) *Froissart*, p. 244.

(132) Oman, *op. cit.*, p. 196.

(133) *Froissart*, pp. 245-6.

(134) Oman, *op. cit.*, p. 198.

(135) Riley, *op. cit.*, p. 450.

(136) *Ibid*, p. 450.

(137) Chaucer, *Canterbury Tales*, p. 245.

(138) *Froissart*, p. 246.

(139) Oman, *op. cit.*, p. 198.

(140) *Froissart*, p. 247.

(141) *Ibid*, p. 247.

(142) Oman, *op. cit.*, p. 199.

(143) *Ibid*, p. 200.

(144) *Froissart*, p. 248.

(145) Oman, *op. cit.*, p. 200.

(146) *Ibid*, p. 200.

(147) *Ibid*, p. 200.

(148) *Ibid*, p. 201.

(149) *Ibid*, p. 201.

(150) *Ibid*, p. 202.

(151) *Froissart*, p. 250.

(152) Oman, *op. cit.*, pp. 202-3.

(153) *Ibid*, p. 203.

(154) *Ibid*, p. 203.

(155) *Ibid*, p. 204.

(156) *Ibid*, p. 205.

(157) *Ibid*, p. 204.

(158) *Ibid*, p. 205.

(159) Dobdon, *op. cit.*, p. 305.

(160) Hughes, *op. cit.*, pp. 234-5.

(161) *Ibid*, p. 234.

(162) Oman, *op. cit.*, p. 97.

(163) Dobson, *op. cit.*, p. 314.

(164) Hughes, *op. cit.*, p. 236.

(165) Dobson, *op. cit.*, p. 287.

(166) *Ibid*, p. 335.

(167) Oman, *op. cit.*, p. 157.

# Index

125

126